Inflation and Unemployment

Inflation and Unemployment

Second Edition

Samuel A. Morley

Professor of Economics
Vanderbilt University

The Dryden Press
Hinsdale, Illinois

(Previous edition was titled:
The Economics of Inflation)

Copyright © 1979 by The Dryden Press

Library of Congress Catalog Card Number: 78-56198
ISBN: 0-03-041016-9

Printed in the United States of America

789 090 987654321

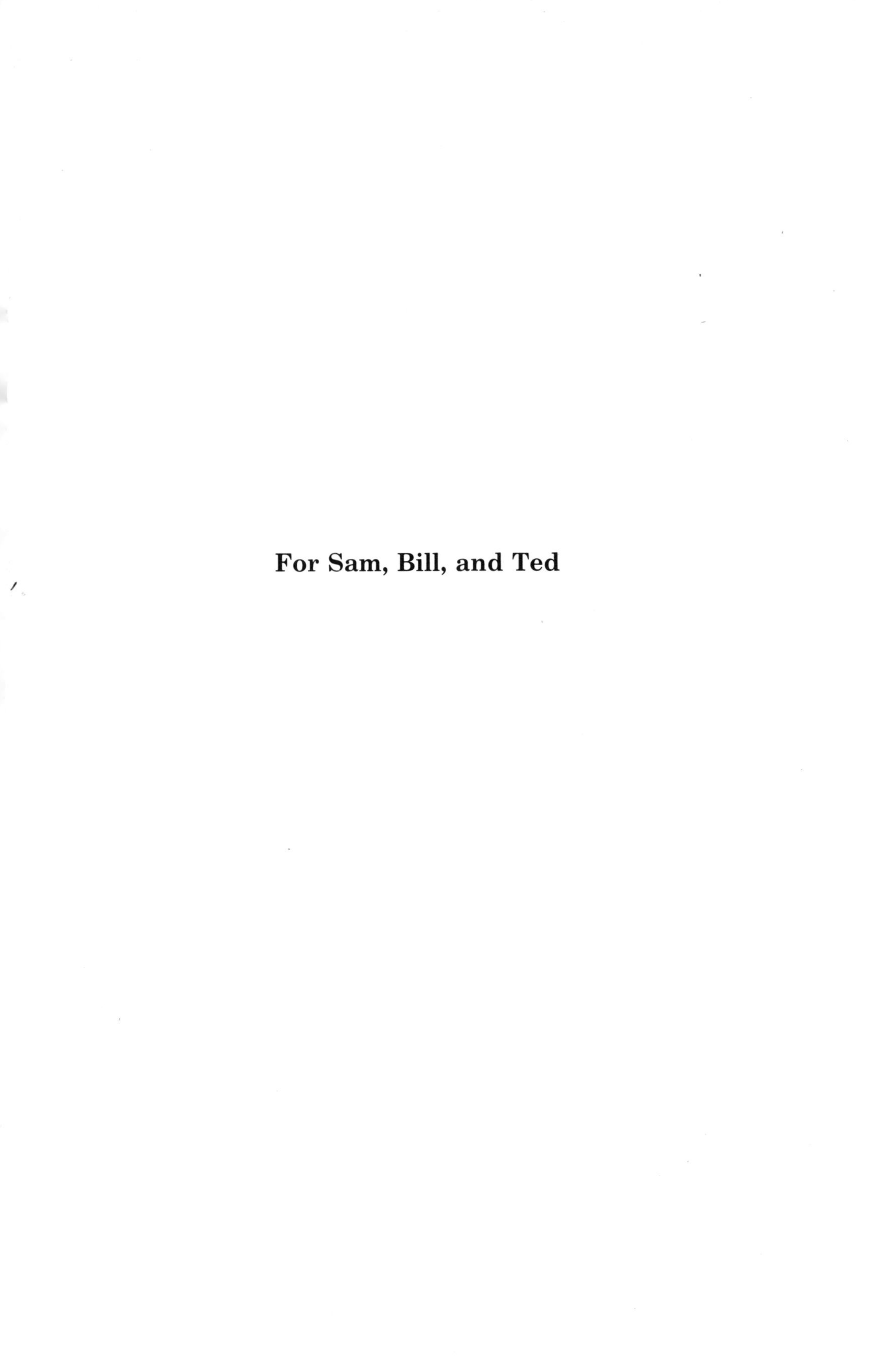

For Sam, Bill, and Ted

Contents

Preface

In the first edition of this book I hoped to provide a supplement to the standard macroeconomics text that would incorporate the most recent (1971) work on the economics of inflation. That work, based on the theory of expectations, provided a good explanation for the gradual acceleration of inflation during the latter half of the 1960s and for the simultaneous rise in inflation and unemployment that followed from government efforts to stabilize the economy in 1968–1969.

Despite the fact that the book was well received, experience with stabilization in the 1970s convinced me that the expectations model on which the earlier book was based is not an adequate explanation for how an economy acts during a stabilization recession. Clearly, prices and wages have been far more resistant to market forces and demand conditions than anyone would have predicted. We need to know why.

Furthermore, the nature and function of unemployment during stabilization are not well described by the expectation theory. According to the theory, unemployment during stabilization is voluntary; it results from workers overforecasting the inflation rate and demanding too high a money wage. But most people's observation is that unemployment is caused not by the refusal to work at the going wage but rather by a shortage of job offers at that wage.

Economists have been actively developing new theories to deal with these anomalous facts. The theories, which focus on the disequilibrium behavior of product and labor markets, suggest that firms may stockpile labor in response to a fall in sales that is expected to be temporary. This, in certain circumstances, implies that wages are insensitive to aggregate levels of unemployment and that prices will not fall with sales.

The theoretical work is still in its preliminary stages. Nonetheless, I feel that it is so helpful in understanding our present stabilization difficulties that it deserves to be included in any macroeconomics course. It is my hope that this book provides a way of doing so as well as an integrated treatment of how economies respond to changes in aggregate demand through movements in prices, output, and employment.

Traditionally, undergraduate macroeconomics courses have focused mainly on demand factors leading to thorough study of monetary and fiscal policy. But I think it is more rewarding for both student and teacher to focus on what is not well understood rather than on what is. In our economy the main policy problems and puzzles lie on the supply side—that is, in the operation of labor markets and aggregate supply curves. Hence, this book attempts to lay out a complete theory of supply and to show how supply and demand factors interact to determine inflation and output. It is written as a supplement or a substitute for the supply section of the standard text. As to level, the book is intended for use in the second half of a one-semester introductory or intermediate course in macroeconomics. It presupposes only knowledge of a basic model of income determination.

My intellectual debts on the subject of inflation are too many to mention specifically. However, I would particularly like to thank Rendigs Fels, Ann McWatters, Donald Wells, and Roger Andreae for their patient reading and constructive comments on the manuscript. Thanks also are due my students here at Vanderbilt. Their interest encouraged me to write, and their comments helped me to clarify my ideas and my presentation. Finally, I would like to thank Elaine Lewis for the patience and care with which she readied this manuscript for publication.

Nashville, Tennessee   S. A. M.
September 1978

Chapter One

Introduction

Inflation is the primary macroeconomic problem facing all Western economies. For most of the last ten years we have unsuccessfully sought a method of returning to a world of stable prices. Yet inflation rates show no sign of diminishing in the United States despite a stabilization program which has generated two recessions and cost at least $400 billion in lost output since 1970. People who have lived through this difficult period do not have to be convinced that inflation is a serious and continuing problem.

The Cause of Inflation

There is now fairly widespread agreement about the cause of inflation, but none at all about how to cure it. Inflation is almost always caused by excess aggregate demand. Generally the excess demand has been generated by too rapid an increase in a nation's money supply. If one looks back at historic price series, four major periods of unreversed increases in prices can be seen. Each is associated with a large increase in the money supply. The first occurred from

1525 to 1650, when the Spanish discovered gold in the New World. The second occurred in the second half of the eighteenth century, at the time of the invention of fractional reserve banking and the resultant expansion of bank or credit money. The third ran from 1932 to 1959, when governments discovered deficit financing and the world was at war. The last is our own period, an inflation which started with the Vietnam War and was accompanied by an explosion in the world money supply due to rising world liquidity and big government deficits.

The association of rising prices with monetary growth was formalized in the quantity theory, whose most recent and sophisticated advocate is Milton Friedman. The quantity theorists assert that no inflation is possible without an expansion in the money supply, that all inflations are caused by excess demand, and that a critical element in controlling inflation is stopping the expansion of money. To the quantity theory we owe the simple (and perhaps simpleminded) notion that inflation is "too much money chasing too few goods." Such inflations should be accompanied by full employment and full use of capacity. Neither men nor machines should be idle.

After both the Vietnam and Korean Wars, however, the United States experienced a different sort of inflation. Prices rose despite substantial unemployment. In the 1950s observers believed that strong labor unions were forcing business to raise its prices to cover cost and they invented the term *cost-push inflation* to describe this phenomenon. In more recent years someone coined the inelegant term *stagflation*. The distinguishing feature of cost-push inflation or stagflation is rising prices despite high rates of unemployment and constant or even declining output.

Economists used to analyze inflations by classifying them as either cost-push or demand-pull, as the excess-demand, full-employment inflation came to be called. Yet there are problems associated with this classification scheme. One difficulty in labeling a particular inflation as either cost-push or demand-pull is that the classification depends upon the starting point. This year's wage increases may be the result of last year's price increases. Labor may be trying to catch up with an unexpected rise in the cost of living, so that the cause of the latter may also be the cause of the former. If one ignores previous years, he will call this year's wage increases evidence of cost-push inflation. But what if those wage boosts are really a delayed reaction to prior inflation? Then all the years are part of a single inflationary process, and it makes no sense to classify separately the causes of increasing prices in any particular year.

A modern view of inflation tends to ignore the distinction between cost-push and demand-pull and to think of inflation as a process with certain characteristic phases. Typically the initial phase, which we call the expansionary phase, will show all the symptoms of demand-pull inflation. Wages are rising, and output and employment are high and probably growing. At some point the economy enters a second phase, in which output and employment level off or fall. But prices and wages still rise, with wages generally rising faster than prices; this phase is called cost-push inflation or stagflation. But we prefer to think of it as the stabilization phase of the inflationary process. It is a typical part of the adjustment by the economy to previous excess demand.

Following this interpretation one could think of the cost-push inflation of the 1950s as the stabilization phase of an inflationary process that began with World War II. That phase was completed by around 1960, when a new expansion began. The 1970s are the stabilization phase of an inflation that began about 1965 with expenditures on the Vietnam War.

One of the principal purposes of this book is to develop a simple economic framework that will generate the two-phase inflationary process. This framework relies heavily on inflation expectations by labor, and has now come to be known as the *expectations model of inflation*. This model offers one plausible explanation for how the inflationary process begins and for what roles are played by excess demand for goods and by labor's wage demands.

Cures for Inflation

If the cause of inflation is excess demand, surely the way to cure inflation is to reduce demand. That is what many economists and most government policymakers believe. In the United States we have spent a large fraction of the last ten years experimenting with policies which reduce aggregate demand in order to stop inflation. Our experience has not been a very happy one.

Most economists were surprised that the extended recessions of the early seventies did not make more of a dent on rising prices. Both prices and wages have a troublesome tendency to be inflexible downward. They appear to be much less sensitive to demand than previously believed. We do not yet know for sure why this is so, but the evidence strongly suggests that it is. A number of explanations are currently being formulated and tested. We will draw on this work to construct a model which implies wage and price rigidity in response to sluggish demand. This model provides an explanation for the largely unsuccessful attempt to stop inflation in the U.S. economy.

I should warn the reader that there is sharp disagreement within the economics profession about the applicability of these new theories of wage and price rigidity, from which stems a profound disagreement about the appropriate way to stop an inflation. Those who believe in flexible prices favor contractionary monetary and/or fiscal policies to reduce demand until the inflation rate gets down to an acceptable level. Those who do not believe in flexible prices think that such contractionary policies cause recessions rather than falling inflation rates. They say, since prices do not react to demand conditions beyond a certain point, there is no use in forcing demand below that point in order to lower inflation rates. Price and wage controls are preferred by this group to fight inflation.

There is no clear winner yet in this theoretical debate. I will objectively present the opposing positions and the evidence supporting them. However, I should say in advance that I think the empirical evidence in favor of rigid prices is so compelling that I cannot help taking a stand and trying to show the reader why I reached my conclusion. If this way of presenting the issues stimulates thought and concentrates attention on the key issue, which is the shape of the aggregate supply curve at less than full employment, this book will have served its purpose.

Suggestions for Further Reading

Ball, R. J., *Inflation and the Theory of Money*. Chicago: Aldine, 1965.

Bronfenbrenner, Martin, and F. D. Holzman, "Survey of Inflation Theory," *American Economic Review* (September 1963), 593-661.

Frisch, Helmut, "Inflation Theory 1963-1975: A 'Second Generation' Survey," *Journal of Economic Literature* (December 1977), 1289-1317.

Gordon, Robert J., "Recent Developments in the Theory of Inflation and Unemployment," *Journal of Monetary Economics* (April 1976), 185-219.

Johnson, H. G., and A. R. Nobay, eds., *The Current Inflation*. London: Macmillan, 1971.

Laidler, David E. W., and Michael J. Parkin, "Inflation: A Survey," *Economic Journal* (December 1975), 741-809.

General Introductory Works on Inflation

Ball, R. J., and Peter Doyle, eds., *Inflation*. Baltimore, Md.: Penguin, 1969.

Flemming, John, *Inflation*. London: Oxford University Press, 1976.

Lerner, Abba P., *Flation*. Baltimore, Md.: Penguin, 1973.

McCulloch, J. Huston, *Money and Inflation: A Monetarist Approach*. New York: Academic Press, 1975.

Solow, Robert M., "The Intelligent Citizen's Guide to Inflation," *The Public Interest* (Fall 1975), 30-66.

Trevithick, J. A., and C. Mulvey, *The Economics of Inflation*. London: Halsted Press, 1975.

Chapter Two

Inflation: Measurement and Costs

Before discussing further the causes of inflation and the dilemmas it poses for policymakers, it is useful to take a closer look at what inflation is, how it can be measured, and why it is considered undesirable.

A Definition of Inflation

What is inflation? The immediate response is rising prices—the working definition we will use in this book. But we can go one step further and ask: what causes those rising prices? This may appear to be an unanswerable question; we are going to argue, however, that rising prices are always caused by excess demand, meaning that buyers would like to buy more than sellers are willing to sell. But, you must be saying, at what prices? There is always excess demand at some set of prices. If the price of Chevrolets falls low enough, eventually the number of buyers will be greater than the number of cars that General Motors is willing to produce. So let us be more precise and say that inflation occurs whenever there is excess demand at last year's prices. That is, buyers would like to buy more than sellers are willing to sell at last year's prices. In such a situation, prices will rise from last year's level to a point where buyers and sellers are agreed on a single quantity that is to be willingly produced and purchased. Whenever there is excess demand, as we have defined it, prices will be rising. Rising prices—inflation—are the symptom of excess demand. With price controls the causal link between excess demand and inflation is broken. Rising prices are replaced by rationing or waiting in lines. Under these circumstances one can learn little by studying the behavior of prices.

Measurement of Inflation

We have been speaking rather glibly about price increases and rates of inflation without worrying too much about measurement. Yet the measurement of rising prices is not simple in a complex economy that produces and consumes many different goods. For a single commodity, we can collect a historical series of prices, and from it can calculate the rate of change in the price of the commodity. If there were only one commodity in the economy, the change in its price would be the rate of inflation. But when many commodities exist, each commodity may have a different rate of price change, and we must find some way of averaging them.

The way we add the various rates of price change to create an aggregate rate of inflation depends upon our use for that information. If we wish to measure the rate at which the cost of living has increased, we will do it differently depending upon whose cost of living is being studied. Clearly the cost of living to an upper-income suburbanite varies with the price of automobiles, lawn fertilizer, and butter. To a ghetto dweller, the cost of buses and subways, rat poison, and margarine may be more important. For each family we are concerned with how the increase in prices has affected its ability to buy commodities. Therefore we need include only those price changes relevant to the family in question, and average them in a manner that reflects their importance.

In a multicommodity world we aggregate by constructing a weighted average of individual price changes. We do so by multiplying each percentage change by the share of its commodity in the consumer budget. For example, consider the following hypothetical consumption price scheme (Table 2.1).

Table 2.1
Consumption in a Simple Economy

		Period Zero	
Commodity	Price	Quantity Produced	Sales
Cars	$2,000	100	$ 200,000
Bread	0.50	1,000,000	500,000
Oranges	0.30	1,000,000	300,000
		Total Consumption —	$1,000,000

		Period One	
Cars	$2,500	110	$ 275,000
Bread	0.60	1,100,000	660,000
Oranges	0.30	1,100,000	330,000
		Total Consumption —	$1,265,000

Cars made up 20 percent of total consumption; bread, 50 percent; and oranges, 30 percent in period zero. We can therefore calculate the change in the cost of living by the following weighted average:

Change in Cost of Living

Commodity	Change in Price	Share		
Cars	(0.25)	x	0.2	= 0.05
Bread	(0.20)	x	0.5	= + 0.10
Oranges	0	x	0.3	= + .0
				0.15

On average, prices have risen by 15 percent during period one in the example. Notice that this does not represent the price behavior of any individual commodity.

What does this 15 percent rate of inflation indicate? It indicates at a glance how much more money is required in period one to buy the period zero bundle of goods. If we multiply the period zero quantities from Table 2.1 by the period one prices, we find that the total dollar expenditure is exactly 15 percent higher.

Commodity	Period One Prices	×	Period Zero Output	=	Money Value of Period Zero Consumption in Period One Prices
Cars	$ 2,500	×	100	=	$ 250,000
+ Bread	0.60	×	1,000,000	—	600,000
+ Oranges	0.30	×	1,000,000	=	300,000
					$1,150,000

It costs \$1.150 million, or 15 percent more, in period one to purchase the same amount of goods that could have been purchased for \$1 million in period zero.[1]

What Price Indices Are

We have learned how to calculate changes in the cost of living, but we do not yet know how to get an aggregate price series itself. What would we learn if we made an average of the prices of cars, bread, and fruit? Would this average price be interesting to us, even if we could construct it? Generally we are more interested in how prices change over time than we are in their absolute level. Thus economists traditionally ignore absolute prices and express prices as percentages of their value in some particular year. Expressing price as a percentage of its base year value converts a price *series* into a price *index*. To construct a price index, we arbitrarily choose a base year and divide the prices in all other years by the price in that base year. The price index shows at a glance the percentage changes in price since the base year. All goods are comparable because all are expressed in terms of percentage deviations from a common base.

The construction of price indices is illustrated in Table 2.2.

[1] The change in the cost of living can be constructed either by taking a weighted average of the individual rates of inflation or by taking the ratio of period one quantities valued at period zero prices divided by period zero quantities at period zero prices minus one. The two methods are algebraically equivalent.

$$\text{INFLATION} = \frac{P_c{}^1 Q_c{}^0 + P_b{}^1 Q_b{}^0 + P_o{}^1 Q_o{}^0 - P_c{}^0 Q_c{}^0 + P_b{}^0 Q_b{}^0 + P_o{}^0 Q_o{}^0}{(P_c{}^0 Q_c{}^0 + P_b{}^0 Q_b{}^0 + P_o{}^0 Q_o{}^0) = \text{CON}^0}$$

$$= \left(\frac{P_c{}^1 - P_c{}^0}{P_c{}^0}\right) \frac{P_c{}^0 Q_c{}^0}{\text{CON}^0} + \left(\frac{P_b{}^1 - P_b{}^0}{P_b{}^0}\right) \frac{P_b{}^0 Q_b{}^0}{\text{CON}^0} + \left(\frac{P_o{}^1 - P_o{}^0}{P_o{}^0}\right) \frac{P_o{}^0 Q_o{}^0}{\text{CON}^0}$$

[CON = Consumption]

Note that the fraction in parentheses is the percentage change in each commodity price and that it is multiplied by the proportion or share of base-period expenditure on the good.

Inflation and Unemployment

Table 2.2
Sample Price Indices

| | Price Series | | Price Indices | |
Year	Cars	Bread		
0	2,000	0.50	100	100
1	2,500	0.60	125	120
2	3,000	0.70	150	140
3	3,200	0.75	160	150

Formally the price index of good i in year j is $P_i{}^j = \dfrac{P_i{}^j}{P_i{}^o} \times 100$, the ratio of the price in year j to the price in the base year.

As one would guess from our previous discussion of aggregation, an aggregate price index is simply a weighted average of individual price indices where the weights are the shares of the individual commodities in the base period.

Difference between Nominal and Deflated Magnitudes

One of the main uses of price indices is to separate changes in economic magnitudes like GNP or aggregate consumption due to changes in prices from those due to changes in production or real purchasing power. For example, we read in the newspapers that GNP in 1976 was $1.7 trillion compared to $750 billion in 1966. Some part of the large increase is only a change in prices, and we use a price index to find out exactly what part. We have already seen that a price index measures change due to price. If, therefore, we divide GNP in 1976 by the GNP price index for 1976, we have 1976 GNP in base period prices. We call this magnitude "real" or deflated GNP, which we will write as GNP_R. Current, or nominal, GNP will be denoted GNP_N. The nominal value of any variable is its value in current money prices, while its real, or deflated, value is its value in terms of the prices of some base period.

Let us refer to our consumption example (Table 2.1). Nominal consumption rose by 26.5 percent in period one. Setting period zero as the base year, the period one price index is 115.[2] Thus, real

$$^2 \qquad P_1 = \left[0.2 \; \frac{2500}{2000} \; + \; 0.5 \; \frac{.60}{.50} \; + \; 0.3 \; \left(\frac{0.30}{30} \right) \right] \times 100$$
$$= 0.2 \; (125) \; + \; 0.5 \, (120) + 0.3 \, (100)$$
$$= 115$$

consumption is $1,265,000/1.15 = $1,100,000. Comparing this with the base period, we see that real consumption has increased by 10 percent. Thus the 26.5 percent increase in nominal consumption resulted from a 15 percent increase in prices and a 10 percent increase in goods purchased ($1.10 \times 1.15 = 1.265$).

We have said that a deflated, or real, variable is the same as current quantities valued at base period prices. Let us see if this is true for our example. We add period one quantities valued at base period prices.

Base Period Prices $\times$ *Period One Quantity* $=$				*Deflated or "Real" Consumption*
C_R $=$	$2,000	$\times$	110 $=$	$220,000
$+$	0.50	$\times$	1,100,000 $=$	550,000
$+$	0.30	$\times$	1,100,000 $=$	330,000
			Total	$1,100,000

The figure $1,100,000 is the amount that would have been spent on consumption in period one if prices had not changed. The example demonstrates that real, or deflated, magnitudes can be obtained either by dividing a current value by a price index or by adding quantities valued in base period prices.

Real values are useful because they tell us about quantities. In 1974 nominal GNP increased by 8.2 percent. But does this tell us that production had increased? No, it does not; for real GNP fell. All that growth was an illusion of rising prices, which one discovers by observing what happened to real GNP.

Price Indices in the United States

In the United States there are three main price indices: the Consumer Price Index (*CPI*), the Wholesale Price Index (*WPI*), and the *GNP deflator*.

The *CPI*, published monthly by the Bureau of Labor Statistics, measures the cost of a market basket of goods and services purchased by an average urban wage earner or clerical worker. Since expenditure patterns change, the weights of the various components of the market basket are periodically updated by means of an extensive consumer survey. The most recent update took place in 1972-73.

The CPI is our most closely watched price index, partly because it measures changes in the cost of living, but also because it is used to escalate wage payments for workers with cost-of-living clauses. More than 8.5 million workers are covered by such agreements as well as all the social security beneficiaries and food stamp recipients.

Many people have criticized the CPI because it is not based on all urban consumers but only on urban wage earners and clerical workers. To remedy this defect the Bureau began publishing a CPI for all urban consumers in February 1978.

The *WPI*, also published monthly by the Bureau of Labor Statistics, is based on the prices of commodities at the wholesale level. It is not a good measure of the cost of living because it does not include services such as health, rent, and education. Furthermore, it counts input prices more than once, thus pyramiding the effects of this price change. For example, a rise in the price of oil shows up directly, then again as a rise in the price of fertilizer and plastic, and finally as a rise in the price of the products using plastics or fertilizers as inputs. Probably indices for individual commodity groups published as subindices of the WPI are more useful than the WPI itself.

The *GNP deflator,* published quarterly, is our best measure of the changing price of currently produced output. Unlike the CPI, this index does not reflect items such as sales taxes, interest rates or the cost of secondhand cars, all of which affect the CPI. It is calculated in a less direct manner than either the CPI or WPI. Each quarter the Department of Commerce calculates the GNP in current and constant dollars. The former is a measure of the flow of output in the economy at current prices. The latter is the same flow, valued at the prices of some base year (the current one is 1972). The GNP deflator is simply the ratio of GNP in current and 1972 dollars. Thus for example, in 1976, GNP at current prices was $1692 billion, whereas at 1972 prices GNP was $1265 billion. The GNP deflator was 1692/1265 − 1.34, which says that the price of produced output had risen by one third between 1972 and 1976.

Costs of Inflation

We now know what inflation is, how it is calculated, how it is reported in the newspapers, and some of the jargon to be used in discussing it. We still do not know if inflation is bad or good, how it is caused, or what it does to an economy. Why is inflation disliked and feared? Is it bad for everyone or only for bankers? These questions concern us next.

No one can afford to be indifferent about the future rate of inflation in a monetary economy. Most contracts—mortgages, labor agreements, bank deposits—are specified in dollars. Inflation is a reduction in the purchasing power of a dollar. Inflation decreases the amount of goods the holder of a dollar may obtain in exchange for the dollar.

One bad thing about inflation is that its impact on different groups is decidedly unequal. A person whose income or assets are fixed in nominal terms loses; those who can adjust the prices of items they have for sale are protected. The person who owes money (a debtor) is at an advantage, because the repayment of debts requires less sacrifice of future goods. By the same token, creditors lose because they are repaid with dollars that will buy fewer goods than when they were lent. People on pensions and holders of government bonds, life insurance policies, or bank deposits are creditors who obviously lose during an inflation. One can regard inflation as a kind of tax which reduces purchasing power, as all taxes do. It is a very discriminatory tax, falling unequally on different groups of taxpayers in the economy.

Another cost of inflation is that it causes the economic system to operate inefficiently. Because inflation may involve income loss, it is reasonable to expect people to try to protect themselves against that possibility. In doing so they devote time and resources which could have been used in leisure or production. For example, people find it costly to hold currency and checking accounts because of the loss in purchasing power as prices rise. They try to get along with less than they would under stable prices by keeping smaller balances and by buying inflation-proof assets with the difference. The motive for holding money is the greater convenience it allows in making transactions. With smaller money holdings, people find they must make more trips to the bank to deposit and withdraw funds. Thus inflation causes a loss of convenience or leisure.

     Inflation and Unemployment

Business also takes steps to protect itself from inflation. It becomes worthwhile to use labor to collect bills more rapidly, because unpaid bills, like any other nominal debt, cause a loss in purchasing power. This same labor could be used to produce things, rather than to reduce inflation-caused financial losses. Thus inflation causes a misallocation of labor, both for the consumer and for business. In an inflation, investors find it profitable to speculate in inventory. The demand for gold coins, stamp collections, and Swiss bank accounts rises, because they are hedges against inflation. This too is unproductive, because the savings could have been used to finance real additions to the capital stock of the economy.

Inflation and Labor

Consider the problem for the worker. Most workers work under contracts that run for one year or longer. Salary levels are agreed upon at the beginning of the contract. To the worker the salary represents the command over goods that one obtains in return for work. The individual is interested in the number of dollars he or she earns, because dollars represent the right to buy a certain quantity of goods and services. The worker does not derive pleasure from owning dollar bills, but is concerned with the number of refrigerators or loaves of bread a day's work will earn. Clearly the number depends on price changes that occur over the life of his/her labor contract. A salary is paid in dollars, and the purchasing power of those dollars changes if there is inflation. The worker cannot, therefore, think only in terms of nominal wage, but must convert earned dollars into an equivalent number of refrigerators and loaves of bread. This is done by deflating or dividing his/her wage by an index that represents his/her cost of living. The real wage, W/P, represents the worker's command over goods. If W/P falls, he or she is working for less in real terms, regardless of how much his/her nominal wage has risen.

As an illustration, suppose a certain group of workers is willing to work for a wage of $2 an hour. Suppose also that the price index is 100, so that W/P is 2.00. The workers, expecting no inflation, sign a one-year contract for an hourly wage of $2. During the course of the year, however, prices rise by 10 percent. By the end of the year, the workers discover that they are actually working for $2.00/1.10 = \$1.80$ an hour. That is, they can buy only as many goods with their $2 wage as they could have bought originally with a wage of $1.80 an hour. The following year the workers demand a return to the real wage of $2, which means a nominal wage of $2.20. Once again they are acting as if they expected no inflation, because if inflation continues at 10 percent, they will find that they were again working for a real wage of less than $2 for most of the year. Income is being redistributed from them to their employers by the inflation, because they did not anticipate it.

Alternatively, if this same group of workers realizes that inflation will recur each year, they will attempt to push their real wage above $2 at the beginning of the year. In that way the real wage will be above its desired level for part of the year and below it for the rest. The two parts should offset each other, so that on average the real wage is at its desired level.

The point is that labor must make some forecast of inflation, and the larger that forecast becomes, the larger the wage increases demanded by labor will be.

Expected Inflation and Financial Markets

Laborers are not the only ones whose behavior is influenced by their forecast of inflation. Expected inflation also has an important impact on the way the public holds its wealth, and thereby on the terms of borrowing. Financial loans are contracts specifying repayment in future dollars. Lenders transfer present purchasing power to borrowers, and they expect the same amount of purchasing power returned to them in the future plus some interest for its use. Like laborers, lenders are not interested in the number of dollars being returned to them, but in the command over resources that the dollars represent. They too must make a forecast of inflation to be expected during the loan period. If prices are rising at 5 percent a year, the lender needs an interest rate of 5 percent just to recover the real value of the money lent. Thus the interest rate charged is likely to be equal to the lender's forecast of inflation plus whatever interest rate would have been charged had no inflation been expected.

Therefore we must make a distinction between real and nominal interest rates, just as we did between real and nominal wages. The nominal interest rate will equal the real rate plus the expected rate of inflation. We should observe a rise in nominal interest rates during inflations, because lenders learn to expect inflation. This may explain a good deal of the variation in the nominal interest rates in the United States in recent years.

Expected inflation induces the public to try to change the composition of its wealth. At any moment there exists a certain stock of money, bonds, equities, houses, and other physical capital. Some of these assets protect the holder against inflation, others do not. When a change is expected in the amount of future inflation, the demand for inflation-proof assets rises and the demand for other assets falls. This will cause the price of inflation-proof assets to rise in relation to the others.

Consider outstanding bonds. Bonds are pieces of paper promising to pay the owner a certain number of dollars in interest each year plus a fixed amount of principal at some specified future time. Once again the holders, or buyers, of that security have the problem of distinguishing between the number of dollars they will receive and the real value of those dollars. Suppose a corporate bond was issued some time in the past when the rate of interest was 5 percent. That bond was sold originally at $1000 and paid yearly interest of $50.[3] During the current year, however, expected inflation has risen by 2 percent, making the current nominal interest rate 7 percent. What happens to the price of our 5 percent bond? Clearly no buyer will pay $1000 to receive a $50 yearly income, because one can earn $70 with that same amount by buying a newly issued bond. Rather, the buyer will pay an amount such that 7 percent of it equals $50 (bond price = $50/.07 = $714). The bond price falls to $714.

The rise in expected inflation costs our bondholders dearly. The market price of their bonds falls by almost 30 percent. To put it another way, whenever the expected rate of inflation rises, all future contracts denominated in current dollars become less attractive as ways of holding wealth, because the store of purchasing power they represent falls. Bonds are a good example of such a contract. Therefore one can expect their price to fall in relation to other assets.

[3] Assume, for simplicity, that the redemption date is far enough in the future that we can ignore the effect of inflation on the repayment of the principal.

The characteristic that makes an asset a good hedge against inflation is its ability to maintain its value in relation to goods, that is, its purchasing power. Bonds do not do this, as we have seen, but durable goods do. As prices go up, relative prices of various physical goods generally remain fairly constant, so the rate of exchange between one good and another does not change. Those who invest their savings in houses, diamonds, or land find that the amount of goods they have to give up to buy their assets is just about the same as the amount they get back when they sell them, regardless of the inflation. Whenever the public's expected rate of inflation rises, therefore, the demand for physical assets should increase and the demand for financial assets should decrease. Because the amount of all these assets is fixed at any moment, an increase in expected inflation should increase the price of the physical assets in relation to the financial ones. A person will be willing to hold the financial assets only when their nominal return is so high that they yield the same real return as physical assets. For bonds, as we have seen, this equilibrium can occur only after there are substantial losses for bondholders. In countries with long histories of rapid inflation, or in hyperinflation, there is a flight from all financial assets into physical goods. It becomes impossible to sell bonds, and the public holds all its savings in the form of land, buildings, cars, or even inventories of canned goods.

Questions

1. What is the difference between the GDP deflator, the WPI, and the CPI? When should each be used?
2. Periodically the government changes the base year for its price indices. Why is this necessary? Can you think of any defects inherent in price indices as measures of your cost of living?

Suggestions for Further Reading

Alchian, Armand A., and B. Klein, "On a Correct Measure of Inflation," *Journal of Money, Credit and Banking* (February 1973), 173-191.

Noe, Nicholas N., and George M. von Furstenberg, "The Upward Bias in the Consumer Price Index due to Substitution," *Journal of Political Economy* (November-December 1972), 1280-1287.

    Inflation and Unemployment

Triplett, Jack, "The Analysis of Domestic Inflation
Measurement," *American Economic Review* (February
1977), 135-141.

Chapter Three
The Labor Market

The labor market is the key to the linkage among aggregate demand, inflation, and the level of output in an economy. It is in this market that most economists have sought an answer to the question of why changes in the level of aggregate demand lead to changes in employment and output rather than prices and wages. Wages and prices appear to be relatively inflexible and insensitive to the level of aggregate demand, at least in the short run. If we knew why, we would be well on our way to understanding why economies have booms and depressions, rather than just inflations and deflations. In this chapter we will describe and compare various theories of the labor market, paying particular attention to the way each of them portrays the response of the labor market to fluctuations in aggregate demand.

A. The Classical Model of the Labor Market

In order to compare more easily alternative labor market theories, it is useful to derive a common analytical framework for the demand and supply of labor. Imagine a world in which all jobs and all workers are homogeneous. What would be the demand for labor in such a world? That is, how much labor would the typical firm be willing to employ at different wage rates? Just like any other buyer, the employer hires labor services (man-hours) so long as their value to him or her is at least as great as their cost. From a knowledge of the production process, the businessperson knows just how many extra widgets an additional worker can produce. Because he or she also knows the price of widgets, it is possible to calculate the extra revenue which will be received from employing an additional person. The businessperson can then compare the cost of that individual to see if it is profitable to hire him or her. The employer is in business to earn maximum profit, and should therefore hire workers only as long as the extra revenue they produce exceeds the wage they must be paid.

The additional revenue generated by each additional person is called marginal revenue product (MRP). It is equal to the marginal physical product of labor (MPP, the number of extra widgets) multiplied by the price of widgets. Therefore the profit-maximizing businessperson follows this simple rule: Make the MRP of the last worker hired just equal to the wage. The firm hires workers until the extra revenue produced by one worker just equals what that worker has to be paid.

$$\text{Maximum profit rule: Wage} = \text{MRP}_{\text{last worker.}} \tag{3.1}$$

If we know the wage rate, the price of widgets, and the schedule of extra widgets produced by extra labor, we should be able to predict how many workers the firm will employ and how many widgets can be produced.

Suppose an individual widget maker produces under the conditions shown below.

Labor Worker-Days	Total Output (Widgets/Day)	MPP (Number of Extra Widgets Produced by Additional Worker)	Price	MRP
1	20	20	$10	$200
2	35	15	10	150
3	45	10	10	100
4	50	5	10	50
5	53	3	10	30
6	55	2	10	20
7	56.5	1.5	10	15

If the wage is $20 a day, the firm following the above rule will hire six workers and will produce 55 widgets. That will maximize total profit—revenue minus labor costs.[1]

The product schedule of the widget firm has what we call diminishing returns. That is, the MPP per extra worker decreases as more workers are hired. Diminishing returns is an assumption, but a number of important results follow from it, so we should understand its rationale. In drawing up our product schedule, we are assuming that fixed capital and management resources are constant. When the firm hires extra labor, the amount of machinery and management per worker falls. Output per worker should depend positively on capital and management per worker, so that the MPP of additional labor declines. Diminishing returns follow from the fact that the supply of machines is constant at any moment of time. Over time, if the firm invests in new machines, the product schedule will rise, allowing the firm to increase employment.

In general, we would expect that the higher the wage, the smaller the demand for labor. This is clearly true for the widget firm. For example, at a wage of $25 per day, the firm would hire only five workers, the reason being diminishing returns. If wages rise, the employer must contract his labor force until MPP increases by an equal amount. If employment is to be increased, either the wage must fall or prices must rise. To say the same thing in another way, the real wage, W/P, must fall.

In Chapter 2 we learned that the real wage is the nominal wage deflated by the price index. W/P is then the rate of exchange between labor and goods—the amount of goods the businessperson has to give up to buy a day of labor. In our example, the real wage is $\$20/\$10 = 2$, or two widgets per day. With this in mind we can now reinterpret equation 3.1; it can be written as:

$$W/P = \text{MPP}_{\text{last worker}}.$$

In other words, our maximum profit rule can be restated: Make the MPP of the last worker hired just equal to the real wage. Furthermore, because MPP decreases as the labor force increases, we know

---

[1] In our example, the firm is indifferent about hiring five or six workers, because the numbers we have presented show the MPP as being equal to two widgets for all levels of employment between five and six.

that the firm will want to increase employment only if the real wage decreases.

We can summarize our discussion by stating that under the assumption of diminishing returns to labor, the relationship between the quantity of labor demanded and the real wage will be negative. This relationship is depicted graphically by the conventional demand curve *DD* shown in Figure 3.1. What *DD* says or represents is that the higher the real wage, the fewer laborers hired; the lower the real wage, the higher the employment.

Our discussion of labor demand has been carried out at the firm level, but the shape of the labor demand curve for the entire economy should be the same. Each firm maximizes profits by hiring labor until the wage of the last worker just equals its MRP. If the demand curve for each firm has the same downward slope, this downward slope is preserved when we aggregate over all firms. We can interpret *DD* in Figure 3.1 as an economy-wide demand curve for labor, which says that employment depends negatively on the real wage. The reason for this is that the capital stock available to the economy is fixed at any moment, as it is for the firm. There are only a certain number of machines available to the labor force, so that the additional product of new employment should be falling. Of course, capital formation by the economy over time will push the labor demand curve to the right, just as it will for the firm.

Supply of Labor

Having discussed the aggregate demand curve for labor, we are left with the problem of the labor supply curve. Before discussing this problem, however, we should distinguish between two different quantities of labor—hours and people. The two will differ whenever hours per day or days per month change. For convenience, we will assume that the number of hours of labor services each worker provides is fixed. We can then translate the business demand for a number of hours of labor services into a demand for a number of workers. Our labor market diagram will then be shown in terms of number of workers employed instead of number of labor hours. This simplifies the analysis and is also defensible in light of the institutional constraints on the ability to

$$\frac{W}{P}$$

Labor

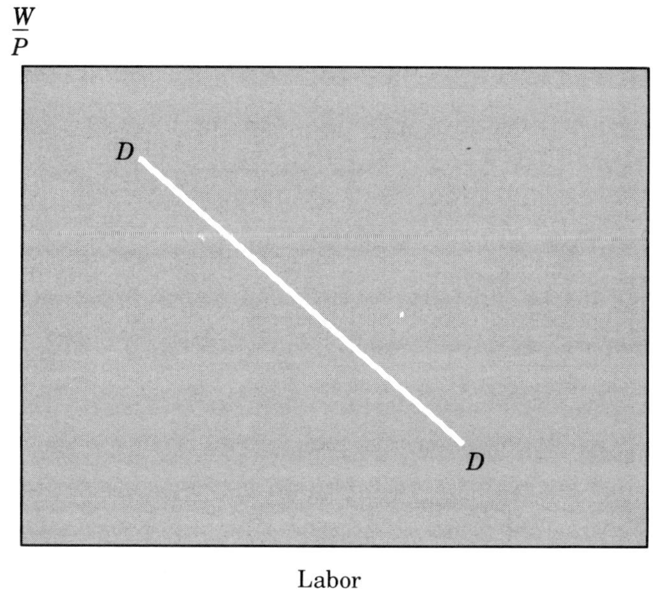

vary the length of the work week or work year in response to wage variations.

Consider now various concepts of labor supply. Labor supply can mean the number of people in the labor force, or the number willing to accept job offers. Hence we have two labor supply curves to derive. The first, the supply curve for the labor force, shows the number of workers in the labor force as a function of the wage. The second, which we will call the supply curve of labor, shows the number of workers willing to work at different wage rates.

Labor contracts are expressed in nominal wages, but we have already claimed that a worker is interested in the command over resources which is gained in exchange for giving up leisure. Dollars are not useful in themselves, but only for what they will buy. The worker should be thinking of the real, not the nominal, wage. The real wage tells exactly how many goods the worker will receive per day of leisure forgone. The labor supply curve, for whatever concept of supply we adopt, should therefore show the relationship between supply and the real wage.

What does the labor force supply curve look like? It might seem natural to expect that a rise in real wages would bring more people into the labor force. After all, the rise in W/P increases the return to work. But most heads of families are not free to enter or leave the labor force in response to wage variations. They may accept unemployment as they look for a better job, but they do not leave the labor force. The source of any potential fluctuations in the size of the labor force must therefore be sought in the secondary labor force.

A rise in real wages may well bring nonworkers into the labor force. It is equally possible, however, that as the real wage of the head of the family rises, part of that extra income is used to buy leisure for family members in the secondary labor force. We have two opposite effects—on the one hand, the rise in real wages makes working more attractive; on the other, it also increases family income and the demand for leisure.

In the absence of any firm conviction or knowledge about which effect dominates, we will assume that one offsets the other. We are thus asserting that a rise in the real wage does not change the number of people in the labor force.[2] In terms of Figure 3.2 we are saying that the labor force supply curve is vertical.

Consider now the labor supply curve. It differs from the labor force supply curve by unemployment. To understand the former curve we must take a closer look at unemployment. What are its economic determinants and what is its economic purpose?

A person is voluntarily unemployed when he or she is in the labor force, but is devoting full time to seeking a better job. The cost of this unemployment is the wages that would have been earned, and the benefit is the higher paying job that might be found by further search. This type of unemployment has been called *frictional* unemployment. It stems from imperfections in the labor market. Jobs and workers are not perfectly alike and information about each is not perfect. Workers have an idea of the real wage they should be able to command, but they do not know where such a job vacancy exists. One way of finding it is to devote full time to a job search. Unemployment is a way of gathering information about the job market in a world where information is costly.

One way of conceptualizing the unemployment decision stems from Phelps.[3] Imagine the economy as a set of separate islands with one factory on each. Information about local island wage rates is perfect, but can be obtained for other islands only by visiting each island and sampling its labor market. In other words, to be certain of the opportunities elsewhere, a worker must leave work and travel around the neighboring islands. When is it rational then for this individual to become unemployed? It is rational only when the worker believes that the future increase in wages to be gained by moving to another island more than compensates for the days of current wages lost through unemployment. In the rarefied world of perfect information and foresight, unemployment would

---

[2]   For further literature and evidence on labor participation rates, see Glen G. Cain, "Unemployment and the Labor Force Participation of Secondary Workers," *Industrial and Labor Relations Review* (January 1967), 275–297, and Belton Fleisher, *Labor Economics: Theory and Evidence*, (Englewood Cliffs, N.J.: Prentice-Hall, 1970), 73–91.

[3]   E. S. Phelps, "Money Wage Dynamics and Labor Market Equilibrium," *Journal of Political Economy* (July–August 1968).

not occur. Each worker on each island would know exactly what his or her opportunities were. Search and unemployment would be irrational, because all wage rates for equivalent work would be equal. Why, for example, would a carpenter ever quit a job to look for a better paying one if there were one economy-wide wage rate for carpenters? Unemployment is rational only where jobs are not all alike and information is not perfect. Unemployment occurs when workers believe they can increase their lifetime earnings by devoting full time to searching for a better paying job. Note that this sort of frictional unemployment is beneficial to labor, because it is a way of increasing earnings in a world of imperfect and costly information. We should also note that frictional unemployment is not a result of low wages per se, but a result of wages being lower than those a person expects to find by looking further.

The frictionally unemployed are a revolving pool of people acquiring information about their opportunities by devoting full time to a search of the job market. They have certain expectations about the level of real wages they desire and should be able to command. The expectations are based upon what other people in the same profession are earning, hearsay, newspaper advertisements, and other factors. These unemployed will be traveling from job opening to job opening, looking for the job that meets their expectations. Presumably, as their period of unemployment becomes longer, they will scale down those expectations until they finally find an acceptable job.

At any point in time, what would it take to reduce the level of frictional unemployment? Remember that each unemployed worker is searching for an acceptable real wage. If there should be a general rise in real wages, some of the unemployed would find jobs and wages meeting or exceeding their expectations. In other words, a rise in the average real wage should reduce the level of frictional unemployment. Conversely, we could say that a rise in the real wage increases the number of people actually working.

We can now summarize all this discussion by completing the labor market diagram. In Figure 3.1 we showed the demand for labor. Now we add two new curves (see Figure 3.2). *LL* is the labor force supply curve. Because, by our assumptions, it is fixed at any point and is not affected by the real wage, it is a vertical line. (The line will be shifting to the right over time, as the labor force expands

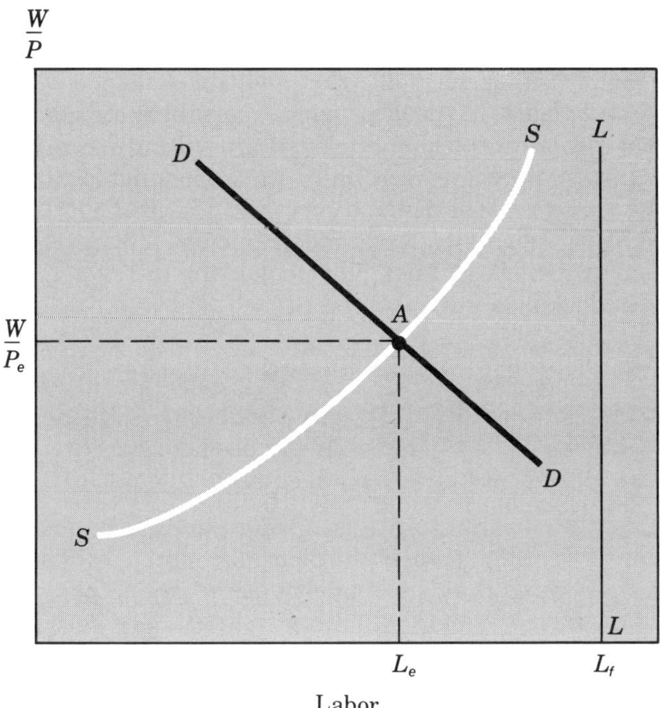

$\dfrac{W}{P}$
D
S
L
A
$\dfrac{W}{P_e}$
S
D
L
L_e
L_f
Labor

along with the population.) SS is the supply curve of labor. It shows the number of people who are willing to work as a function of the real wage. The distance between SS and LL is voluntary frictional unemployment. SS is upward sloping, because of our assertion that as real wages rise, more and more of the unemployed find wage offers in line with their expectations and accept jobs.

Equilibrium in any market is defined as a state in which the quantity supplied equals the quantity demanded or where the market clears. In the labor market, equilibrium will occur at that real wage rate at which employers are willing to hire all the people willing to work. Geometrically, we are looking for a point on both the supply and the demand curves. In Figure 3.2, this is obviously point A, the intersection of the two curves. At that equilibrium, employment is L_e, unemployment is the distance L_f-L_e, and the real wage is W/P_e.

If the real wage were lower, there would be an excess demand for labor. Some jobs would be unfilled, because jobholders would have left work to seek higher wages elsewhere. As business tries to fill the vacancies, it will be forced to raise its wage offers. The process will continue until the real wage rises to its equilibrium level W/P_e.

It may seem surprising to the reader that unemployment exists in equilibrium. Isn't unemployment a symptom of disequilibrium? Keep in mind that the unemployment here is the voluntary frictional unemployment, which occurs in a large heterogeneous labor market where job changes cannot take place instantaneously. This has been labeled by economists as the normal or equilibrium unemployment level and estimated at between 4 percent and 5 percent of the labor force for the United States. Equilibrium unemployment differs fundamentally from the larger amounts of unemployment that occur during serious recessions as we shall now see.

Up to this point there is little disagreement among economists about the analysis of the labor market that we have presented. The problems only begin to arise when we ask what happens in the economy and in the labor market when there are variations in aggregate demand. How can we explain the persistence of unemployment in excess of the normal amount during depressions? Why is employment positively related to aggregate demand? Economists have been struggling with these questions ever since the depression of the 1930s produced unemployment for one out of every four members of the labor force. The search for answers has intensified with the upturn in unemployment since

1970. Clearly the unemployment record of most economies in the last fifty years is not predictable by the simple labor market model we have presented above. Let us consider now three important attempts to provide better models or explanations.

B. The Keynesian Labor Market Model

Keynes made two key empirical points in his analysis of the labor market. The first is that wage bargains are made in nominal or money terms rather than in real terms. Workers may think in real terms, but labor contracts are not written that way except in some recent cases where cost-of-living clauses are included. This seemingly simple fact has far-reaching implications for macroeconomic equilibrium, if workers do not react immediately to price level changes. For example, suppose that workers have a contract to work for $5 per hour when the price index is 100. If they continue to work for $5 even when the price index rises to 125, then their real wage has declined to $4, and they are supplying the same amount of labor as before at a lower real wage. In terms of diagram 3.2, the labor supply curve has shifted vertically downward. The level of prices in the economy influences the position of the labor supply curve *if,* and this is a crucial if, labor does not change its wage demand whenever the price level changes. An increase in demand which raises prices will shift the labor supply curve down, thus raising employment; a fall in prices will shift the supply curve up and reduce employment. Thus we see that *if* workers do not react to price changes, changes in aggregate demand will lead to changes in employment and output, as well as changes in prices.

Keynes's second main point was that workers are exceedingly reluctant to allow their nominal wages to decline. Wages, he claimed, are inflexible downward. Furthermore, he thought that workers were more likely to resist a reduction in money wages with prices fixed than an equivalent reduction in real wages which resulted from a rise in prices with money wages constant. In view of our discussion of the determinants of labor supply, it may seem irrational for labor to distinguish between these two situations since both lead to the same real wage. However, Keynes did not see this distinction as irrational at all. The money wages of different labor groups determine the distribution of labor income. For one labor union to accede to a reduction in money wages would mean a fall in its relative position within the labor force. An equivalent decline in real wages resulting from a rise in prices affects all workers equally. It reduces real income, but does not affect the distribution of income among workers. Downward rigidity of wages stems from the importance of the distribution of income to members of the labor force.

We now incorporate these two assertions about the labor market into the labor market diagram. Because of wage rigidity, the Keynesian labor supply curve will be horizontal rather than upward sloping. Because money wages do not respond fully to price movements, the position of the supply curve will depend on the price level.

In Figure 3.3 we show two such Keynesian supply curves. The first is drawn for an equilibrium money wage W_e and a price level P_e. It is horizontal to the left of employment level L_e to represent the fact that the labor force will not accept a reduction in the money wage, W_e. At point A, the supply curve has a kink. This represents the assumption that workers will accept a rise in money wages, even if they won't accept a reduction. Beyond point A, the Keynesian labor supply curve follows the supply curve of Figure 3.2.

At the price level P_e, equilibrium in the labor market is at point A. There the real wage is W_e/P_e and L_e workers are employed. At this point, unemployment is the distance L_e-L_f. This is exactly the same frictional unemployment that we have seen in Figure 3.2.

Suppose now that aggregate demand in the economy declines, forcing prices to fall from P_e to P_1. To the left of A, workers refuse to accept a reduction in wages. They are ready to work for a wage of W_e, but not for less. However, that money wage now represents a higher real wage because of the decline in prices. In effect workers are demanding a higher real wage than before. The supply curve shifts vertically upward to the curve labeled S', moving equilibrium from point A to B, the intersection of S' with the labor demand curve. As the reader can see, employment drops from L_e to L_1, and unemployment rises by the same amount. Thus the fall in aggregate demand has led to a rise in unemployment and a reduction in real output.

The great contribution of the Keynesian analysis was the development of a theory which could account for large quantities of

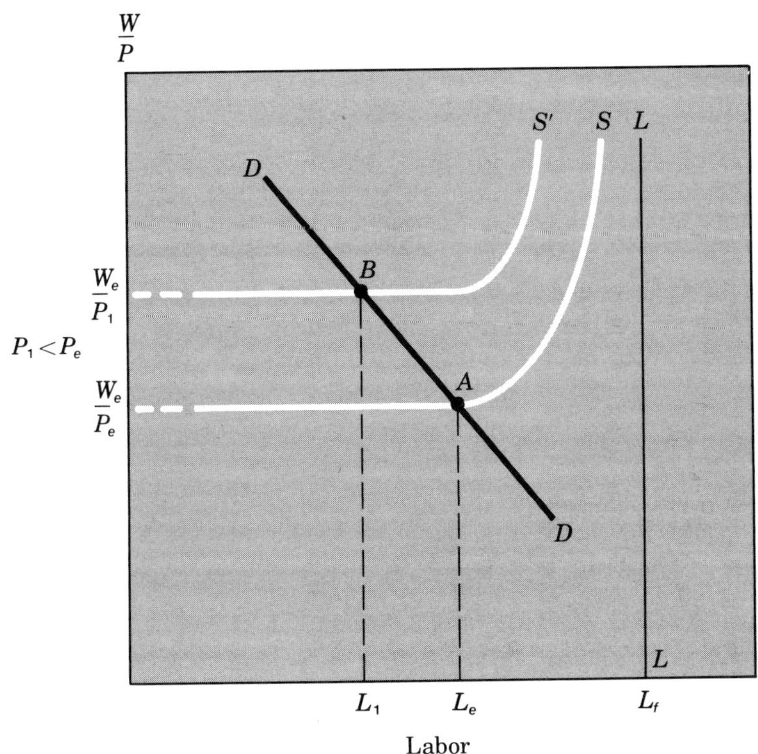

 The Labor Market

unemployment. Keynes wanted to distinguish sharply this sort of unemployment from the voluntary or frictional unemployment that we have analyzed before. He called it *involuntary*, which he defined as any unemployment which would be reduced by a rise in the price level, holding money wages constant. For him, involuntary unemployment was the result of too low a level of aggregate demand.

Many critics of the Keynesian analysis contested the idea that such unemployment was involuntary or that it resulted from a lack of aggregate demand. After all, they argued, if the labor force would accept a reduction in money wages equal to any reduction in prices caused by a fall in demand, there need be no involuntary unemployment. For these critics, the high rates of unemployment were a result of wage rigidity in the face of fluctuations in aggregate demand, not the fluctuations themselves. Logically the critics were correct, but Keynes had little patience with their point of view. The fact of the matter, he insisted, is that money wages are sticky downward because labor resists wage cuts. That fact should be accepted as one of the behavioral laws of a modern market economy. Once one does that, involuntary unemployment is attributable to inadequate demand. To blame it on wage rigidity would be a little like blaming the law of gravity when a glass falls instead of blaming the person who dropped it.

What would be required to eliminate unemployment? Keynes acknowledged that perhaps an economy would get back to full employment if workers allowed their wages to fall far enough, although he was doubtful. But would it not be ever so much faster and more direct to increase aggregate demand instead through expansionary monetary or fiscal policy?

If wages are inflexible, an important policy issue must be faced. It is this: unemployment will be created whenever aggregate demand falls relative to the money wage. Should the government wait for the unemployed to put pressure on wages? Is involuntary unemployment self-correcting or isn't it? How fast do wages and prices adjust downward? The Classical economists insisted that, given time, the system would get back to full employment without intervention. But as Keynes looked around the scarred world of the 1930s, he thought it absurd or irrational to wait for these self-correcting wage mechanisms in the economy. They were too weak and slow. It would be preferable, he thought, to use monetary and fiscal policy to offset the fluctuations in aggregate demand that brought on the unemployment in the first place. Thus Keynes's view of the labor market led him to espouse an active role for the government in demand management. His advice was to tailor the level of aggregate demand to the historic money wage rate rather than wait for money wages to adjust to a lower level of demand.

C. Neoclassical Search Theories of the Labor Market

The labor market model of Keynes was designed to explain the existence of unemployment beyond the frictional or equilibrium level. His was a model for an economy suffering from insufficient aggregate demand. He was not particularly concerned with economies with excess demand. His model showed why output and employment fell when aggregate demand declined; it had an explanation for depressions. But did it have an explanation for booms? Not really. It was not until the boom period of the 1960s that several economists combined a search theory of unemployment and an expectations model of inflation to provide us with a logical explanation of how economies react to growing aggregate demand. The two names most linked with these theoretical developments are Milton Friedman and Edmund Phelps. The question they set out to resolve was the following: Why do economies have booms when aggregate demand goes up? Why doesn't such an increase simply drive up prices? That is exactly the opposite side of the question Keynes was addressing in the recession. Really it is the same puzzle. If workers and businesspeople both think in real terms, how can a change in prices possibly lead to a change in employment? It should lead to nothing more than a change in money wages by the same percentage amount. Yet, observation in the 1960s, just as in the 1930s, suggested that employment is positively related to aggregate demand. The two are not independent as the Classical model of the labor market says they should be.

The Friedman-Phelps (hereafter F-P) model of the labor market adds expected inflation to the model of unemployment that we developed in section A. Recall that unemployment was a result of the heterogeneity of workers and jobs. Workers voluntarily accept unemployment as a way of obtaining information about the labor market by devoting full time to job search. The model we sketched out was rather hazy about how the prices of goods are determined and how they are perceived by employers and workers. Yet these perceptions are crucial, if both employers and employees think in terms of the real wage rate, rather than the nominal. In the next chapter we will analyze the determination of the aggregate price level in detail. We note here that the labor market model of section A implicitly has assumed that everyone knows the equilibrium price level, and can therefore immediately convert any nominal wage into a real wage. If everyone has perfect foresight about present and future inflation rates, no one will regret his decision. But what if those forecasts are wrong?

In the real world, labor contracts often cover a long period. They require forecasts of price changes for more than one market period. Auto workers sign two-year contracts; steel and aluminum workers sign three-year contracts. Even one-year contracts require price forecasts. F-P argue that the forecasting problem is more difficult for labor than it is for the firm, because the relevant price to the firm is the price of its product, one single price in a market it knows well. Labor, however, has to worry about the entire cost of living. Remember that workers are interested in the general purchasing power of their wage and they calculate this by deflating their money wage by a general cost-of-living index. They have to forecast the prices of housing, medical services, food, and all the other products they use. Management has to forecast only one price. In the F-P world, laborers accept job offers contingent upon what they think the real wage is and will be. Yet they probably have a very dim perception of the path of future prices throughout the economy. It is therefore entirely possible that when the future arrives, there will be a difference between the real wage they once thought they would earn and the one they actually earn. In the real world, there is no reason to assume that labor and management base their plans on the same set of price forecasts. There could thus be a difference between the labor supply and demand curves as perceived by management and labor. What occurs in the labor market when these elements of realism are introduced?

The Effect of Unexpected Inflation on Employment

We are going to trace the adjustment to unexpected inflation by the labor market. To do this, we must distinguish between what we will call the long-run labor supply curve, which is the supply curve when labor's expectations are accurate, and the short-run labor supply curve in which expected and actual prices may be different.

The labor supply curve that we derived in section A shows the amount of labor which will work at different real wages, under the assumption that labor forecasts prices correctly. We are going to call that a long-run curve because, in the short run, labor may make forecasting errors. What we will call the short-run labor supply curve is a relation which shows the real wage at which various numbers of workers are willing to work when there are forecasting errors. The difference between the two curves results from the difference between expected and actual prices. Short-run equilibrium is always at the intersection of the short-run labor supply curve and the labor demand curve.

To see the effect of forecasting errors on the labor market, imagine an economy in equilibrium with constant prices, disturbed by an unexpected rise in government spending. As we shall see, this will cause a rise in prices throughout the economy. Let us suppose that this inflation is entirely unexpected by labor, which forecasts a continuation of the previous equilibrium price level. Each un-employed worker is searching for an acceptable wage offer. He or she is deflating that wage offer by a forecast price level. If no inflation is expected, the prices used are the equilibrium prices of the previous year. But if, unexpectedly, prices are rising (that is, if there is unexpected inflation), there will be a difference between what the real wage is perceived to be and the actual real wage represented by any nominal wage offer. Labor acts on what it perceives the real wage to be.

Thus we amend our diagram of the labor market to include the short-run labor supply curve, S_{SR}, in addition to our original sup-ply curve S_{LR} (Figure 3.4). Whenever prices rise unexpectedly, S_{SR} lies below S_{LR}. L_0 people will continue to work at the old nominal wage even though the rise in prices has reduced the purchasing power that wage represents. It is as if, suddenly, labor is willing to work for lower real wages.

Suppose that previously the labor market equilibrium was at L_0. Now, owing to the shift in the short-run labor supply curve, em-ployment rises to L_1. Why does that occur? The inflation fools some workers. Take the extra workers between L_0 and L_1. This represents the many people who leave unemployment and go to work, because they receive the increase in nominal wages which they sought. They do not, however, realize that this increase is being more than offset by rising prices. Management finds that actual real wages are lower and is able to hire more workers, while the workers think, incorrectly as it turns out, that real wages have risen. Unexpected inflation thus appears to be a costless way of increasing employment.

We can imagine how the rise in prices causes the increase in employment or the decrease in unemployment. The frictionally unemployed have certain nominal wages at which they are willing to work. If prices are rising, employers can afford to raise the nominal wages they pay and the unemployed workers are likely to find an acceptable wage offer and take a job. The rise in prices has reduced frictional unemployment.

Observe carefully what is taking place. The government spending program causes a rise in prices, increased employment, and a fall in real wages. Consider how this process works at the individual factory. Take our widget firm, for example. At the price of $10 and a wage rate of $20, we saw that the factory employed six workers. Suppose that the price of widgets rises to $13.33 and the wage remains at $20. The MRP of any worker will then have risen, producing the revised MRP schedule shown below.

Labor	MRP
4	$66.50
5	40.00
6	26.67
7	20.00

By the rule of equating the wage to the MRP of the last worker, it is now profitable to employ the seventh worker. The unexpected rise in prices allows for an increase in employment because it shifts the short-run labor supply curve down and to the right.

The F-P theory has an explanation for booms: they arise from unexpected inflation. The theory also has an explanation for recessions and what economists call stagflations (i.e., inflation accompanied by high rates of unemployment). They come from workers overforecasting the price level. To see how this will affect the

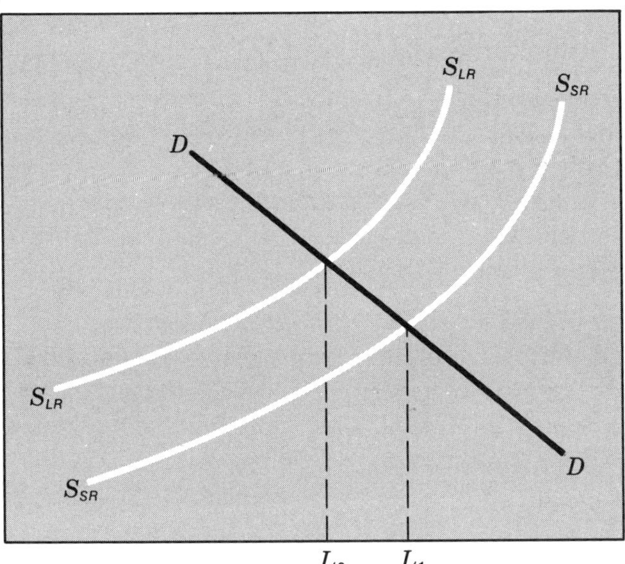

W/P
S_LR
S_SR
D
S_LR
S_SR
D
L_0
L_1
Labor (number of workers)

short-run equilibrium employment level let us return to the economy portrayed in Figure 3.4. Suppose that the long-run equilibrium was disturbed by a fall rather than an increase in demand. Suppose further that this reduction in demand leads to a fall in the price level which is entirely unexpected by labor. What happens to the short-run labor supply curve?

Each unemployed worker is searching for a job at an acceptable real wage. But because of the unexpected price reductions, each worker's nominal wage demand now represents a higher real wage. Without realizing it, the labor force has raised its real wage demands. Because of the fall in prices, the nominal wage required to induce an unemployed worker to accept a job now represents a larger real wage. In Figure 3.5 we show the short-run labor supply curve when labor overforecasts the price level. It lies above and to the left of the long-run labor supply curve.

As before, short-run equilibrium is at the intersection of the short-run labor supply curve and the demand curve. As the reader can see, the unforeseen reduction in demand and prices leads to a reduction in employment. Thus, as in the Keynesian model, a reduction in aggregate demand leads to a reduction in output and employment.

We can summarize all of this discussion by stating the following rule: Whenever prices are higher than workers expect them to be, the short-run labor supply curve will lie below the long-run curve and employment will be higher than the long-run level. Whenever actual prices are less than workers expect them to be, the short-run curve will lie above the long-run curve and employment will be below its long-run level. Whenever labor forecasts the price level accurately, employment will be exactly equal to its long-run equilibrium level. The three rules are represented in Figures 3.6.

These rules are not affected by the actual rate of inflation. Suppose, for example, that the labor force expects a 6 percent rate of inflation, and the actual rate is 6 percent. This is an accurate forecast, and the rule would predict that employment would therefore be at the long-run level. To anticipate a bit, suppose that the actual inflation is 5 percent but workers expect 6 percent. Here workers are overforecasting the price level. Expected prices are higher than actual prices which, according to the rule, means that employment will be lower than the long-run equilibrium level.

Figure 3.5
Labor Market When Expected Price Level Is
Greater Than Actual Price Level

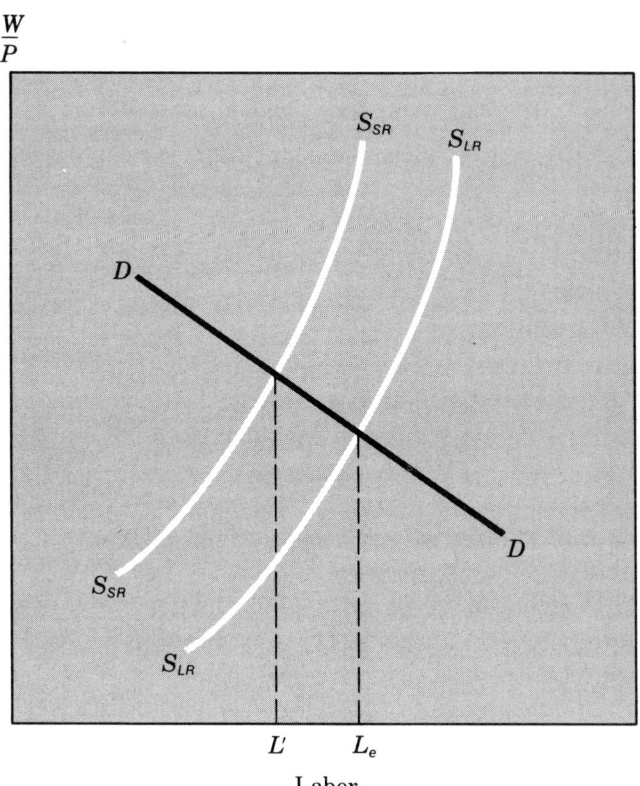

This is high unemployment coupled with inflation—the stagflation of recent years. In other words, the rules could be restated in terms of inflation rates as follows: When workers overforecast the inflation rate, regardless of what that rate is, the short-run supply curve will lie above the long-run curve, and employment will be less than normal. Whenever the inflation rate is underforecast (i.e., whenever there is unexpected inflation), the reverse occurs. The short-run supply curve lies below the long-run curve and there is a higher than normal level of employment. Finally, whenever the inflation rate is correctly forecast, regardless of what that rate is, the long-run curve applies, and employment will be at the normal long-run level. Indeed we might define long-run equilibrium, as F-P did, by the requirement that expected and actual price levels be equal.

While the expected price level is an important influence in the F-P economy, we have not yet considered how expectations are formed. Indeed this is a subject we do not know too much about, because expectations are not directly observable. Most economists, however, believe that expected inflation is some sort of weighted average of actual past inflation rates with a correction for significant current influences, such as oil embargoes, crop failures, the availability of foreign exchange or the government's determination to fight inflation. In general, it is probably true that actual rates of inflation of the recent past play a most important part in forming expectations.

Whenever historical experience is a major determinant of expectations, an economy will be slow to adjust to changes in reality, and the short-run adjustments by the system will be in quantities such as employment and output as well as in prices. To anticipate our story somewhat, the slow adjustment of expectations to changes in the rate of inflation in the F-P model explains very well the typical cyclic pattern observed in the U.S. economy over the 1950s and 1960s. At the beginning of both cycles, prices were stable and the initial rounds of inflation came as a surprise. We will call this first round the expansion phase of the inflationary process. Expected inflation is less than actual inflation, a situation that results in a rise in employment as we have seen. But at some point, the government steps in to control the inflation. However, by this time, the public may expect the inflation to continue. If governmental actions are successful, they reduce the actual rate of in-

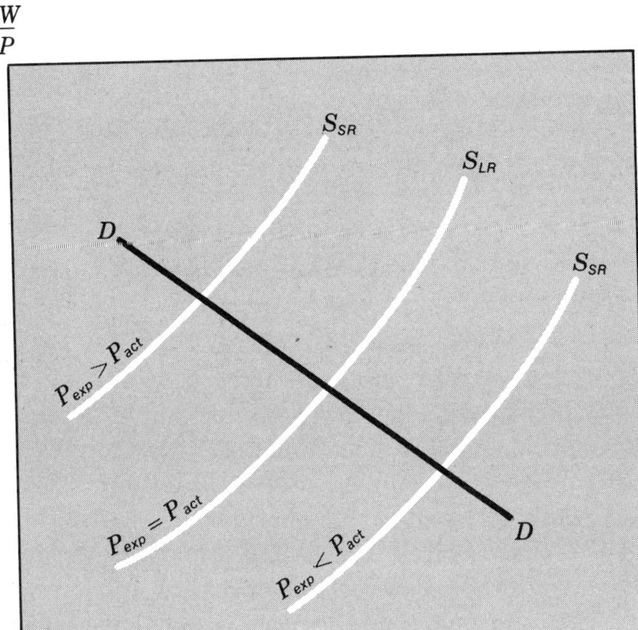

W/P
S_SR
S_LR
S_SR
D
P_exp > P_act
P_exp = P_act
P_exp < P_act
D
Labor

flation, perhaps below what people expect it to be. But, when actual inflation is less than expected inflation, employment falls below its long-run equilibrium level. This is the stabilization phase of an inflation. Because inflation is less than expected during stabilization, one should expect low levels of employment, while high levels should accompany the expansion phase. Both deviations stem from a difference between what labor expects prices to be and what they actually are. Thus the F-P model predicts that fluctuations in aggregate demand will lead to variations in output and employment. They are due to imperfect foresight which can be explained by the expectations lag.

D. Empirical Observations which are Difficult to Explain with the Keynesian and the Neoclassical (F-P) Labor Market Models

As we have seen already, the Keynesian model of the labor market did not have a very good explanation for booms. It seems to be a convincing representation of depressions only. Friedman and Phelps came forward with an integrated model which purported to explain both booms and depressions within a Neoclassical framework with short-run forecasting errors. Their model predicted well the cycles in inflation and unemployment up to the early 1970s. However, the persistent inflation and high unemployment rates in the U.S. economy, starting around 1970, have led a number of observers to question the F-P model and to propose an alternative.

Probably the main difficulty in the F-P model is its characterization of unemployment. For F-P, all unemployment is voluntary. The model implies that the high current unemployment rates are due to the refusal of workers to accept jobs principally because the wage rates are mistakenly deflated by too high a price index. Recessions occur when workers overpredict the price index, causing them to turn down nominal wage offers that they would accept had they been correctly informed about prices. That, to many, is not a very accurate description of the labor market of our days. Most of the unemployed do not have an opportunity to turn down job offers at too low a money wage. Wages are inflexible, but during recessions, employers are simply not hiring at those wages. They do not lower the wage if a queue of unemployed workers appears outside their gates, but they do not hire either. Unemployed workers do not have the opportunity to make a decision about whether the money wage is too high or too low. The evidence points to job rationing at the going money wage, not voluntary unemployment.

A further empirical contradiction of the Neoclassical model is the behavior of quits. Workers quit a job when they anticipate a better job elsewhere. According to the theory, workers overforecast the price level during recessions. The unemployed refuse jobs because they think the money wage is too low. It would be consistent to expect the employed to think the same thing. They would believe that their money wages were not rising fast enough. The "quit rate" should therefore rise in recessions and fall in booms. But of course it does exactly the opposite. Quits fall during recessions, because employed workers know that there are few alternative job opportunities available, while the opposite occurs during booms.

Another important discrepancy between fact and theory is the relationship between employment and the real wage. In all three of the models we have considered so far, short-run equilibrium is always at the intersection of the short-run labor supply curve and the labor demand curve. Employers are always on their demand curve. Since the labor demand curve is downward sloping, a fall in real wages is required to increase employment. Yet evidence has been accumulating for years which shows unmistakably that real wages and employment are positively correlated, not negatively as the theory predicts. Both go up in booms and down in recessions.

What we have are continuing major anomalies, which are not well explained by the two main labor market theories presently being used by economists. They are: job rationing during recessions, the behavior of quit rates over the cycle, and the positive historical correlation between real wage rates, employment and the level of economic activity. These have led a number of economists to propose alternative theories which might be consistent with the above anomalous facts. These theories are still in the formative stage, but the work appears to be sufficiently promising to merit an extended description. We turn now to that description.

E. Internal Labor Market Theories

An explanation for most of the discordant facts noted above can be generated by a combination of internal labor market theories and price rigidity. According to the internal labor market theory (hereafter ILM), labor is not homogeneous, but differentiated according to acquired skills. Some skills, such as reading, are perfectly general—that is, transferable between jobs. Other skills are *specific*, that is, useful only in the particular job. Williamson has labeled such jobs idiosyncratic.[4] Examples of such jobs might be the operation of a unique machine or the supervision of a particular, unusual group of employees.

How do individuals acquire the skills required by different sorts of jobs? Where the skills are general, they can be economically taught in schools outside the firm. In contrast, the skills required by idiosyncratic jobs probably can only be acquired at the workplace, either through on-the-job training or by observation. Either individuals are hired and learn how to do their jobs while doing them (badly at first), or other employees learn how to do a job by watching it being done or perhaps even by doing it on a temporary basis. Such employees are natural replacements when vacancies occur.

Thus the effect of skill specificity is to segment labor markets. Idiosyncratic jobs tend to be staffed by employees already at the firm. Outsiders may not even be considered. Presumably the reason for this is that employees can acquire the specific skills required for an idiosyncratic job at a fraction of the effort and time required of an outsider. The labor market for idiosyncratic jobs tends to be intrafirm or internal.

Of course workers are idiosyncratic too. Another important feature leading to internal labor markets is the cost of acquiring information about the employee. Many jobs require a high degree of honesty, cooperation, leadership or judgment. These are qualities which are hard for a firm to evaluate objectively, and hard to predict through job interviews. An alternative is to use a job promotion sequence as a screening device. This seems to be particularly important for supervisory and money-handling positions. Internal or firm-specific labor markets are thus a natural development serving to minimize the cost of information transfer about jobs and employees when both are heterogeneous. This seg-

---

[4] O. E. Williamson, M.L. Wachter, and J. Harris, "Understanding the Employment Relation: The Analysis of Idiosyncratic Exchange," *The Bell Journal of Economics*, 6 (Spring 1975), 250–278.

mentation of labor markets has important implications for wage
flexibility as we shall see below.

Firm-specific skills help explain the strong linkage between most
workers and their employer. For a variety of reasons, it appears
that most workers and firms enter into a longer-term relationship
than the standard labor market model implies. There is a fairly
strong reluctance on both sides to sever this relationship. The
reason is firm-specific job skills. For the worker, a job is more than
simply a chance to exchange work for a salary. It also provides the
opportunity to learn new job skills, either about his or her own job
or about others at the firm. Some jobs, therefore, provide entree to
an attractive sequence of future jobs. In such cases, the employee
has a strong motivation to remain with the firm. Lifetime earning
prospects at the firm should be higher than they would be in
another firm because of the specific skills that have been learned,
and also because the firm has learned about the employee. By
leaving the firm, one loses the promotion possibilities and all the
firm-specific skills that have been acquired on the job.

Skill specificity, as we see, creates a presumption that employees
will stay with their firms. The converse is also true. Employees
should become more valuable to the firm the longer they work. Let
us see why. Where employee skills are specific—useless outside
the particular firm—it is reasonable to expect that training costs
would at least partially be paid for by the firm. Trainees would
receive a salary higher than their marginal product during training, which the firm would hope to recoup by paying a salary lower
than marginal product over the trainees' future working life at the
firm. Thus, specifically trained people should be worth more to the
firm than they are paid, and the firm suffers a capital loss if such
people quit. The loss is compounded where employees acquire
knowledge about other jobs in the firm as they perform their own
jobs; for this makes firm employees more trainable and capable of
filling vacancies at low cost.

To summarize, when firm-specific skills and information about
employees are important, we should observe a strong attachment
between the firm and the worker. Valuable knowledge is lost
whenever this attachment is broken, either through quitting or
through firing. For our purposes here, the main implication of this
is in terms of what is called *labor stockpiling*. Stockpiling means

the <u>continued</u> employment of workers at a firm even though production levels do not require their presence. Clearly labor stockpiling of employees with firm-specific skills is rational for a firm
which faces a temporary reduction in demand, since it would have
to train a new set of laborers when sales returned to normal levels.
If a firm has a multiperiod time horizon, it will accept short-run
losses by retaining its skilled labor force in the face of temporary
reductions in sales.

We should add here that labor stockpiling may also result from
restrictive conditions in labor contracts rather than intertemporal
cost minimization. Whatever the cause, stockpiling implies a
positive relationship between output and labor productivity. Output per worker will rise in booms and fall in recessions. Empiri-
cally, studies of labor productivity show exactly this pattern,
which is strong evidence in support of the stockpiling theory.

Another observation which is consistent with the long-run link
between workers and firms is the behavior of layoffs and quits.
Feldstein[5] in a recent paper points out that firms tend to lay off
workers rather than fire them. For example, more than 75 percent
of the workers laid off in manufacturing during the last decade
were eventually rehired by their original employer. Furthermore,
a high percentage of the unemployed did not seek another job.
Feldstein was interested in why layoffs were used rather than
reductions in hours worked or salaries. He hypothesized that the
reason may be the existence of unemployment insurance in our
economy. Unemployment insurance provides a subsidy to temporary unemployment which, under current arrangements, will be
preferred by employees to a reduction in hours worked. This institutional arrangement helps preserve the bond between the employer and his employee. That such a high percentage of even those
who are laid off return to their original employer is strong evidence
indeed of the importance of this bond.

The willingness to retain employees, when their presence is not
justified by sales, varies with their long-run value to the firm.
There is little cost in losing employees with low or general skills,
because there is little training cost to acquiring a new employee

---

⁵ M. Feldstein, "Temporary Layoffs in the Theory of Unemploy-
ment," *Journal of Political Economy*, 84 (October 1976), 937–959.

when demand expands. We might therefore expect that fluctuations in aggregate demand would have a differential effect upon the labor force. Dismissals would be negatively related to the level and specificity of the skills possessed by different groups of employees. Fluctuations in aggregate demand will have a highly uneven and regressive impact on the labor force if this theory is correct. Those with little training will be the first fired, and they will be the last to find jobs, as we shall see below.

Another major implication of the internal labor market theories is the idea that wages go with jobs, not with individuals, and are likely to be inflexible downward even when there is substantial unemployment or idle labor at the firm. Economists have assumed that, in the presence of unemployment, wages should fall. Presumably their reasoning is that unemployed workers will offer to work for a lower wage than the firm's own labor force, and the firm will either accept their offer or use it to lower its own wage rate. But if labor markets are segmented, there is little direct competition between employees and outside job applicants. Where employees have specific skills, they may be cheaper to retain than to replace, even if the unemployed substitutes offer to work for less. This has the highly important implication that the unemployed exert less downward pressure on wages, the more widespread are firm-specific or internal labor markets.

But internal labor markets alone do not satisfactorily explain why a firm would not use the presence of external unemployment to force down its own wage rate. There is surely little risk that workers would quit rather than accept a slight cut in salary. Yet observation suggests that firms do not lower their wage rates in response to external unemployment. Okun has recently proposed an explanation for this.[6] He argues that firms try to establish a permanent quasi-contractual understanding with their labor force. The goal is to reduce turnover so as to maximize the creation and retention of skills in order to reduce training costs. Workers are risk-averse and are attracted to firms which offer the prospect of stable employment with rising wages. In a multiperiod model, it is shown that a firm can reduce its labor cost by not allowing wages

---

[6]   A. Okun, "Inflation: Its Mechanics and Welfare Costs," *Brookings Papers on Economic Activity*, 2 (1975), 351 – 390.

to fluctuate with demand. Rather than lowering wages, firms tend to temporarily lay off workers with the understanding that those workers will be rehired as soon as demand conditions permit. Temporary layoffs are preferred to wage reductions by workers, because of the value of leisure time and the existence of unemployment insurance. Furthermore, as Okun puts it: "The firm has clean hands in the case of a layoff; since it is not using the worker, it cannot be 'taking advantage' of him."[7]

To summarize this discussion, when there is a reduction in aggregate demand leading to a decline in sales and a rise in unemployment, firms tend to hold wages constant, and stockpile labor. To the extent that firms cut labor costs, they do so by temporary layoffs and not by wage cuts.

The modifications in firm behavior that we have been considering here dramatically change the analysis of the labor market that was presented in sections A– C. Recall that we derived the demand curve for labor by using a profit maximization rule, which implies that the firm should hire until the real wage of the last worker is just equal to his or her marginal product. This demand curve for labor is not affected by the level of aggregate demand in the economy because of an implicit assumption that the firm can always sell what a worker produces by lowering prices if necessary. What is important to the firm is only the relative price of labor and goods, that is, the real wage. Product prices are assumed to be flexible. But what if they aren't? Then a reduction in aggregate demand must lead to a reduction in output and employment. If for some reason product prices are not flexible, the demand for labor is a function of product demand—that is, depends on things like the money supply, government spending and taxes. It may come as a surprise to the reader, but economists do not, in general, believe that labor demand depends on these macroeconomic variables.

Before turning to the substantial arguments in support of inflexible prices, let us redraw our labor market diagram to show the effect of rigid prices on labor demand. The labor supply function in Figure 3.7 is unaffected by the modifications. It is the same as that in Figure 3.1. Curve *DD* shows the marginal physical product of

---

[7] *Ibid.*, p. 369.

Figure 3.7
Labor Demand Under Inflexible Prices

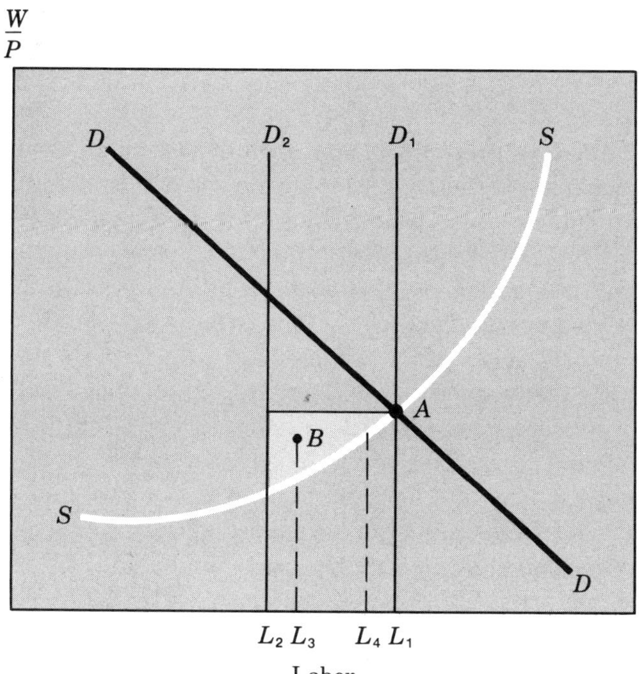

various different quantities of labor. However, because of price inflexibility, we can no longer assume that the labor market will find its way to a point on that curve, except by accident. The two vertical curves D_1 and D_2 show the minimum amount of labor required to produce two different amounts of output Q_1 and Q_2. Clearly Q_2 is less than Q_1. When aggregate demand is such that Q_1 is demanded, labor requirements are L_1. If demand falls to Q_2, labor requirements fall to L_2. In this way labor demand depends on aggregate demand.[8]

Curve D_1 represents an equilibrium position in the labor market. Demand is sufficient to employ the entire labor force at a real wage equal to marginal productivity. But what happens if demand falls to D_2? Labor requirements fall to L_2. However, if there is labor stockpiling, employment does not fall as far as L_2. Excess labor is carried by the firm. If that is so, what wage should the firm pay? Our original theory was very clear—the firm would be willing to pay a real wage equal to the marginal product of labor. But if the firm keeps more labor than it needs, expecting the reduction in demand to be temporary, it cannot pay marginal product. The wage policy is undefined. However, for the reasons discussed above, there is reason to expect substantial wage stickiness. Wages are likely to remain close to their equilibrium level, at least temporarily. While we cannot analytically derive an equilibrium wage and employment level for the new lower level of aggregate demand, we are led to expect that wages and employment will fall somewhere in the shaded area of Figure 3.7. The more layoffs are used to cut labor costs, the closer to L_2 the point will be; the more rigid wages are, the closer to the top of the area.

Under the labor market conditions in a certain economy, suppose the final position is at B (Figure 3.7). B is not an equilibrium point. Neither workers nor firms are happy. For workers there is involuntary unemployment in the amount $L_4 - L_3$. These are people who would like to work at the going wage. The situation is scarcely better for firms. They have more workers than they need, to be exact, $L_3 - L_2$ of excess labor. They are paying wages above labor's marginal product and will suffer a reduction in profits. In effect,

---

[8] R. Barro and H. Grossman, "A General Disequilibrium Model of Income and Employment," *American Economic Review*, 61 (March 1971), 82– 93.

they are paying for the retention of their labor force. The reduction in demand is costly to both labor and business. As we have said, point B is not an equilibrium. Involuntarily unemployed workers tend to put downward pressure on wages, and business is under pressure to reduce its excess labor force. Both of these influences tend to move the economy toward the intersection of D_2 with the labor supply curve. However, that point is not an equilibrium either. Business would be making an excessive profit because the marginal product of the labor force would be greater than the wage it is paid. This would induce firms to expand output and employment by lowering prices for their output. However, this carries us out of our depth in this chapter and we defer discussion of pricing to Chapter 4. The point is that over time the economy should return to the full equilibrium point A (Figure 3.7). However, no one knows for sure how long that might take.

The analysis behind diagram 3.7 is fundamentally different from either the Classical, the Neoclassical or the Keynesian models of the labor market. Here for the first time, short-run equilibrium may be at points off the labor demand curve because of labor stockpiling and price rigidity. Important policy implications follow from this difference. First and foremost, in the internal labor market model, at points like B in Figure 3.7, business simply will not be hiring. It already has more labor than it needs, so it will not hire more, even if new applicants offer to work for less. There is job rationing, and nothing that unemployed labor does will remedy the situation. In both the other labor market models we have studied, unemployment could always be eliminated by a reduction in real wage demands (i.e., employment is increased by moving down the labor demand curve). To my mind, the ILM model more closely fits labor market facts. In recessions business is not hiring. In some long-run sense unemployment may be caused by real wage demands that are too high. But in the short run, employment will not be increased by labor's willingness to work for less. It will be increased only by a direct stimulus to aggregate demands or by goods prices being lowered, for these measures will push D_2 to the right. And note that even here, it may take a substantial increase in aggregate demand before business will start to hire. Only when the demand curve reaches B in diagram 3.6 will employment begin to rise. Thus when there is labor stockpiling, one should expect a rather sluggish response of employment in the first stages of recovery. This is certainly consistent with the historical experience of the U.S. economy.

It should be emphasized that the foregoing analysis was based on the assumption that product prices are inflexible downward. As we saw, if prices fully reflect real wage reductions, labor demand is independent of product demand. If prices are rigid, labor demand is a series of vertical lines in the labor market diagram. There is unfortunately little theoretical reason to choose one or the other extreme. Undoubtedly, the actual situation in our economy is somewhere between the extremes of rigidity and perfect flexibility. This means that the actual labor demand curves lie somewhere between the vertical lines and the downward sloping marginal product curve DD of Figure 3.6. More to the point, they are a function of aggregate demand. This changes nothing in our analysis of labor market reactions to falling demand except the magnitude of the wage and employment reductions. In the short run, the labor market will still drift off the marginal product curve DD into the shaded area where labor stockpiling, wages in excess of marginal product, and job rationing will all be observed.

So far we have analyzed the effects of reductions in demand on labor markets with ILM characteristics. Will the same analysis hold up for expansions? To the left of point A in Figure 3.8, there is no particular problem as the economy is simply moving back to full equilibrium. But suppose that demand continues to increase at A? Suppose that the economy overshoots? If prices are inflexible upward as well as downward, labor demand will be the dashed line D_2. Equilibrium will be at C, the intersection of D_2 and labor supply. At point C, real wages have been raised to attract the additional workers needed to increase output. Indeed real wages are higher than the marginal product of labor, because of diminishing returns. If prices are constant under diminishing returns, therefore, expansions should reduce profits. This prediction, however, is inconsistent with actual experience during booms. Profits have always risen sharply during booms, which is sufficient grounds to reject the hypothesis that prices are inflexible upward as well as downward.

It seems, therefore, that we need a different model for expansions and contractions. For contractions, to the left of the full employment equilibrium point A, the inflexible price model seems to be

Figure 3.8
Excess Demand in the Internal Labor Market

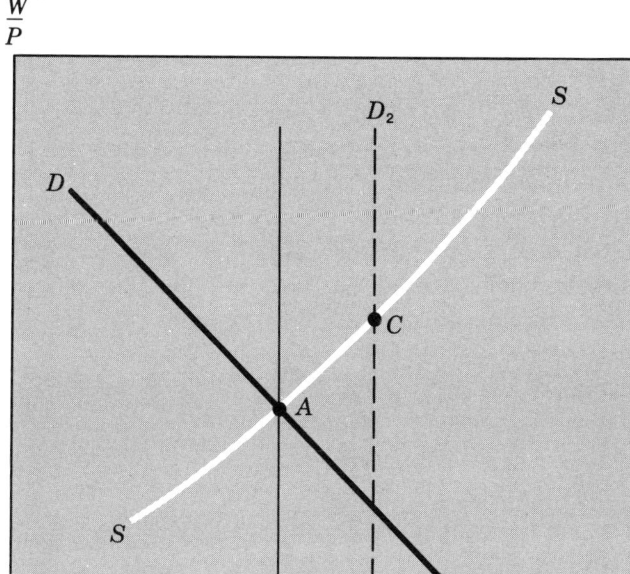

consistent with the observed labor market facts. To the right of A, assume that prices are flexible. What we are saying here is that businesses raise their prices fully in response to cost pressures, but may not lower them. In the next chapter, we will see that one of the reasons why these prices are not lowered is that a pricing model based on costs has been used. With labor stockpiling, labor costs may not decline when aggregate demand falls. In fact they probably rise.

This leaves us with only one problem. If indeed prices are flexible upward, beyond some hypothetical full employment point like A, we cannot use shifts in labor demand to explain employment booms. Beyond A, with flexible prices, we must be on the marginal product curve DD (Figure 3.9). To cover this case, go back to the Neoclassical F-P explanation of the effect of unexpected inflation on labor supply. When demand increases, business raises its prices. In the short run, we will assume that these price increases are unexpected by labor. Then, as we have already shown, the labor supply curve will shift outward from S to S' (Figure 3.9), and employment will increase from the equilibrium level L_e to what could be called the super-full employment level L_s. Real wages decline and the profit share rises as we will see in a later chapter.

To summarize, the ILM theory is a story about how the labor market functions at less than full employment. It gives an explanation for labor stockpiling, rigid wages, differential unemployment rates, and job rationing. Key elements in the model are rigid prices, firm-specific labor markets, and the importance of specific skills. Although the model appears to account for many features observed in depressed, real world labor markets, it must be amended for booms. We choose the Neoclassical unexpected inflation model for this purpose, because its predictions about the labor market in boom periods seem to agree closely with the observable facts. We are saying that labor markets work differently when there are small and large amounts of unemployment. At bottom the reason for this difference is that the firm must decide how much of its skilled labor force to carry over when there is slack, even though some of that labor is superfluous in the short run. That is a rational strategy for the firm, if its labor force has acquired skills which would be costly to replace. But it means that wages do not equal marginal product in a recession. Employers are off their demand curves, and they will not be hiring regardless of

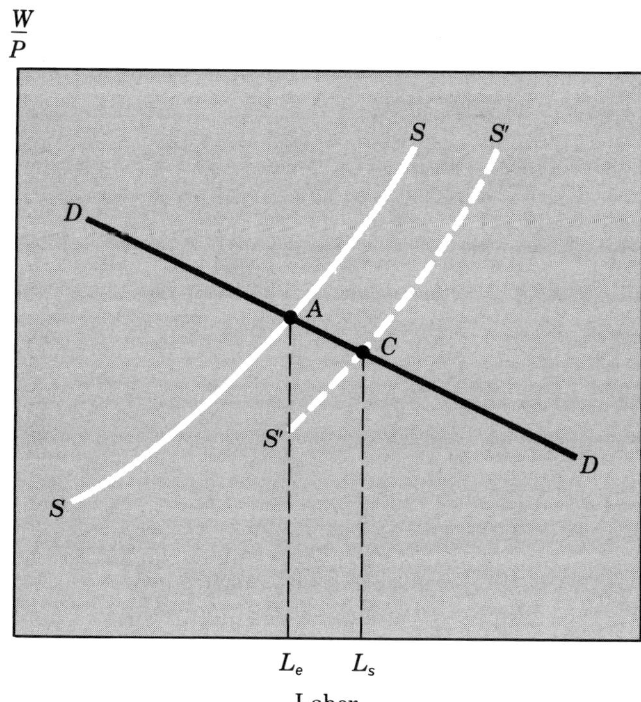

W/P
D
S
S'
A
C
S'
D
S
Le
Ls
Labor

the wage offers of unemployed workers. By contrast, when the economy moves past the normal full employment output, prices do tend to rise. In the short run this may "fool" the labor force, lowering the real wage and increasing employment. However, to complete this model, we must now turn to the goods market where the price level and aggregate demand are set.

Questions

1. What is the difference between the long-run and short-run supply curves in the expectations model? When do the two curves diverge?
2. Why is the downward sloping labor demand curve not relevant if goods prices are rigid?
3. What empirical observations seem inconsistent with the expectations and Keynesian models of the labor market?
4. Why, in the long run, does a change in the price level have no effect on equilibrium employment in the labor market?
5. Is it ever rational for a person to enter the ranks of the unemployed voluntarily?
   a. Under what circumstances would he or she do this?
   b. Could we expect a rational, but unemployed, person to turn down job offers? Why?
   c. How might the decision to accept or to leave a job be affected by either anticipated or unanticipated inflation?
6. Under what conditions would we expect to find an increase in the money wage associated with a decrease in the quantity of labor demanded? with an increase in the quantity of labor demanded? with no change?

Suggestions for Further Reading

Barro, Robert, and Herschel Grossman, *Money, Employment and Inflation*. Cambridge: Cambridge University Press, 1976.

Doeringer, Peter B., and Michael J. Piore, *Internal Labor Markets and Manpower Analysis*. Lexington, Mass.: Heath, 1971.

Friedman, Milton, "The Role of Monetary Policy," *American Economic Review* (March 1968), 1–17.

Gordon, Donald F., "A Neo-classical Theory of Keynesian

Unemployment," *Economic Inquiry* (December 1974), 431–459.

Phelps, Edmund S., *Inflation Policy and Unemployment Theory*. New York: Norton, 1972.

Wachter, Michael L., "The Primary and Secondary Labor Market Mechanism: A Critique of the Dual Approach," *Brookings Papers on Economic Activity*, 3 (1974), 637–680.

Chapter Four

Inflation and the Goods Market

In Chapter 3 we studied the process by which employment and wages are determined. In this chapter we carry the analysis to the goods market, meaning the market for producible output. Here we show how the price and quantity of output are determined in an economy and the effect of changes in aggregate demand. Equilibrium employment and real wage are found in the labor market at the intersection of the labor supply and demand curve. We can use the same procedure in the goods market. We derive goods supply and demand curves, and their intersection determines aggregate output and the price level. As we shall see, different views of the labor market lead to alternative shapes for the aggregate supply curve in the goods market.

Supply of and Demand for Individual Commodities

Let us examine the supply and the demand curves for individual commodities. Consider the beef market. The higher the price of beef, the more the ranchers are likely to produce. Because labor, hay, and fencing costs are still unchanged, it is going to be profitable to raise more cows or to feed each cow more so that it raises a heavier calf. On the demand side, as the price of beef rises, consumers switch to other kinds of meat; as the price falls, they buy more beef. Notice that we are making a key assumption; namely, that only the price of beef changes, while all other prices are constant. Under that assumption, the supply curve in the individual market should be upward sloping, the demand curve downward sloping. The higher the price, the more the producers are willing to supply and the less the buyers are willing to buy.

Aggregate Demand and Supply

To simplify the analysis, assume that only one commodity is produced by the economy. The output of this good is equal to GNP, and changes in its price are the aggregate rate of inflation. What do the aggregate supply and demand curves look like?

Going from the analysis for an individual good to that for the aggregate is not as simple as may appear. Consider demand first. What occurs to aggregate demand when all prices change? Suppose prices for all goods rise by 10 percent. You may think the answer is obvious: Of course demand will fall. But why will it fall? Suppose that the output of each good stays the same, even though prices rise; aggregate income will then rise by 10 percent. With nominal income 10 percent higher, why will people not be willing to pay 10 percent more for the same quantity of goods?

Consider our argument for the individual market. Demand falls for beef as prices rise, precisely because all other prices stay the same. If chicken, pork, fish, bread, and all other prices rise at exactly the same rate and if the consumer's income rises as well, it is difficult to argue that the consumer will buy less beef or any other product. In short, if everything rises at exactly the same rate as prices, there is no reason to suppose that rising aggregate prices decrease aggregate demand.

A change in prices that has no effect on any real, deflated variable should have no effect on demand. Such a change is similar to a government decree making ten old dollars equal to one new dollar—simply a change in units of account. But the rise in prices in an economy does have real effects. It is not the same as a change in units of account. It is like a government decree stating that henceforth one dollar will buy what 90 cents used to buy. The reason the two changes are different is because a rise in prices affects the distribution of income and the real value of savings, both of which affect aggregate demand.

Consider people who hold their savings in the form of currency and government bonds. These assets represent a certain command over resources which we find by deflating the nominal value by the price index. As prices rise, the real value of currency and government bonds falls. Holders of government debt are hurt by the rise in prices. There is a wealth effect. These people now have to save more to compensate for their loss of purchasing power, and their consumption demand should fall as prices rise. Because consumption is part of the aggregate demand for goods, this wealth effect is one reason that rising prices reduce aggregate demand.[1]

A rise in prices should raise the rate of interest and should reduce investment. Briefly, the interest rate is determined by the tastes of wealth holders and the portfolio of assets available to be held. A rise in prices changes that composition, because certain assets rise in price while others do not. Houses, machines, and other real goods rise in price; financial assets, such as bonds, bank deposits, and currency, do not. A rise in prices thus reduces the real purchasing power represented by financial assets, particularly money. Economists have presented quite convincing evidence that the rate of interest varies inversely with the real supply of money. Because rising prices reduce the real supply of money, interest rates should rise.

Continuing this interest rate effect, economic theory states that rising interest rates reduce the demand for capital and lower fixed investment in the short run. The financial effect of rising prices is a rise in interest rates and a drop in investment. Note that all this

---

[1] It could be argued that we should not include government bonds in the wealth effect, because the real value of the future tax liability for repayment of the bonds falls with rising prices. The reduction in future taxes could just offset the loss of purchasing power on the bonds.

assumes that present inflation does not change expectations about future price changes. If it did, we would have to distinguish between the nominal interest rate and the real interest rate. A rise in prices can reduce investment only if it raises the real interest rate.

Another reason that inflation reduces aggregate demand is that it changes the distribution of income, both within the private sector and between the private sector and the government. Both may affect the demand for consumption goods. Consider first the inflationary redistribution within the private sector. It is generally believed that inflation helps profits and hurts wages. The evidence from the U.S. economy suggests that inflation at the beginning of expansionary cycles does indeed shift the distribution of income away from labor. If profit earners have less propensity to consume than labor, transferring income from the latter to the former will reduce aggregate consumption. The same argument can be used for other transfers. Debtors generally gain during an inflation; creditors lose—because debts are specified in dollars. Rising prices change the real purchasing power represented by those dollars. To the extent that debtors have lower spending propensities than creditors, this transfer will again reduce aggregate consumption.

To our minds a more significant transfer is from the private sector to the government through progressive taxes. Income taxes are specified in dollars, and the rates are progressive. Furthermore, the exemptions are expressed in nominal terms. As prices go up, the exemptions become lower and lower in real terms. An increase in nominal income exactly offset by an increase in prices pushes taxpayers into higher tax brackets with higher tax rates. A greater proportion of this income must be paid to the government as prices rise. Using actual U.S. tax rates, an individual with a taxable income of $20,000 pays a tax of $4098. Now suppose that prices and nominal income both rise by 10 percent. This individual's nominal taxable income is now $22,000 and his tax is $4736. In real terms (at prices of the initial year), taxes rise from $4098 to $4736/1.10 = $4305. In other words, the tax receipts of the government rise by more than the cost of living, because the tax system is progressive.

A good example of the effect of inflation on real tax receipts may be seen in the year 1974. During that year personal income rose by 8 percent, but personal income taxes rose by 15 percent. This rise in real tax burden was not caused by a surtax; it was simply the effect of 10 percent inflation on a tax system whose provisions are written in nominal terms.

To recapitulate, we have found three reasons why rising prices reduce demand. The first reason could be called a wealth effect; the second, an interest rate effect; and the third, a redistribution effect. All three occur because price changes have real effects on the distribution of assets and income in the economy, a factor that changes aggregate behavior. There is nothing diabolical or bad in such a situation. A rise in prices should reduce demand.

The Aggregate Supply Curve of the Economy

Consider now the shape of the aggregate supply curve. What would happen to output if prices of all goods changed? In Chapter 3 we saw how a firm was able to increase employment and output when its selling price rose. We reproduce the relevant part of the production table for this firm as it illustrates the process by which price changes affect output in the goods market.

Labor	Total Units of Output	MPP	MRP at $P = \$10$	MRP at $P = \$13.33$
5	53.0	3.0	$30.00	$40.00
6	55.0	2.0	20.00	26.67
7	56.5	1.5	15.00	20.00

With a wage rate of $20 per day and a widget price of $10, the firm hires six workers and produces 55 widgets. When prices rise by 33.3 percent, it becomes profitable to increase production to 56½ widgets, because the rise in prices offsets the decline in MPP of the seventh worker. This conclusion should be fairly general. For any firm where the marginal output of additional workers drops, an increase in selling prices enables it to increase output. In other words, we are showing what occurs to output if prices of all goods change while wages remain constant.

If the price of labor rises just as fast as prices, there can be no increase in output. Consider our widget makers. At a wage of $20 and a selling price of $13.33, they increase their output to 56½ widgets. But what if workers demand a 33⅓ percent increase in wages to compensate for the increase in prices? The new nominal wage rate will be \$22.67, but the profit-maximizing output is still 55 widgets. In other words, when nominal wages are allowed to change along with the prices so that real wages are constant, price changes no longer allow firms to change their output.

Is it reasonable to suppose that wages would change with prices? That depends on our view of the labor market. In the Classical labor market model of Chapter 3, workers are interested in the real purchasing power represented by any nominal wage. Labor supply in Figure 3.2 is drawn in terms of the real wage, not the nominal wage. One should expect, therefore, that for a Classical labor market any change in the price of goods will cause an equivalent change in the money wage rate. Under these conditions, prices will have no relationship to output. Only where money wage demands do not fully reflect changing prices will inflation have any effect on aggregate supply.

The Neoclassical expectations model that we developed in section C of the previous chapter implies a very different supply relationship. According to that model, there may be expectation lags or forecasting errors by labor. When that happens, a change in prices need not lead to an equivalent change in money wage demands because the price change is not perceived by labor. We showed how unexpected inflation allows firms to raise their money wage offers, and how this leads to an increase in employment, because the frictionally unemployed are temporarily fooled into believing that the rise in money wages is also a rise in real wages. What is relevant to the goods market is that when employment rises, so does output. When a rise in prices is unexpected, therefore, both employment and output will increase. Conversely, if prices drop unexpectedly, employment and output will fall.

As in the labor market, we can summarize our discussion of demand and supply in the form of a picture of the relationship between output and prices along the aggregate demand and supply curves (see Figure 4.1). We have already shown that aggregate demand falls with rising prices. Therefore, the demand curve DD has a negative slope. There are two supply curves. The one corresponding to the Classical labor market is the vertical line $S_{classical}$. It shows the amount of output which can be produced by the equilibrium number of workers in the labor market, assuming perfect foresight.

Figure 4.1
Aggregate Goods Market

Price

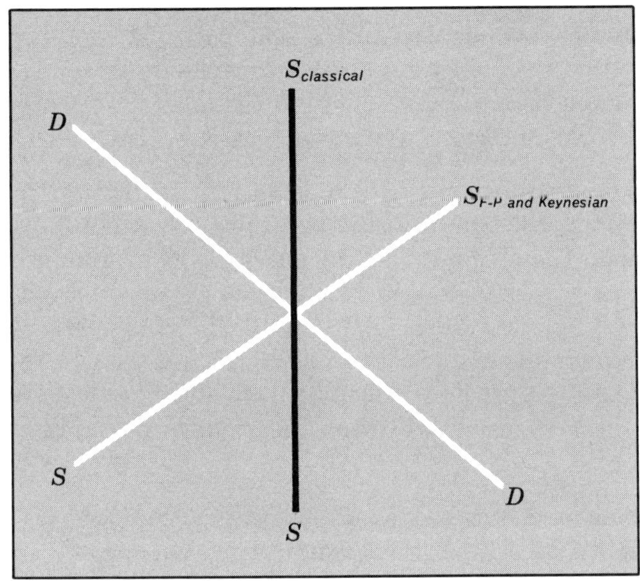

Real Income

The upward sloping supply curve represents both the Neoclassical (F-P) and Keynesian models of the labor market. Let us see why. The supply curve shows the amount of output which will be produced at different price levels. For the F-P model, we showed in Chapter 3 that a rise in prices, if unexpected by labor, would lead to a rise in employment and therefore in output. The F-P upward sloping supply curve should therefore be interpreted as the relationship between output and prices, holding the level of expected prices constant. There is thus a different short-run curve for every different expected price level, and each curve intersects the vertical long-run curve at its expected price level.

This same upward sloping supply is implied by the Keynesian labor market model, although the curve might have a different slope. Recall that in the Keynesian model labor refuses to allow its money wage to decline. Under those circumstances a reduction in demand, which causes prices to fall, leads to a reduction in output because the real wage rises. Falling prices coupled with a constant money wage lead to a decline in employment and output. That is exactly what the upward sloping supply curve in Figure 4.1 represents.

Many economists think of the classical conditions of perfect foresight as a long-run equilibrium condition, and of the expectations and Keynesian models as short run. In the short run, they argue, price forecasts may be wrong and wages may be rigid downward, but these should be temporary conditions. If workers really do think in real terms, prices should have no effect on employment or output in the long run. Only an increase in real productivity through capital formation can do that. One could therefore interpret the vertical supply curve corresponding to the Classical model as a long-run supply curve and the upward sloping curve as a short-run curve.

We are left with the task of drawing the aggregate supply curve corresponding to the ILM model of the labor market. This task is not a trivial one, because we hypothesized that the labor market may not be on either the labor supply or demand curve. Consequently we have no underlying equilibrium conditions to help determine the short-run relationship between price and output. For example, the short-run aggregate supply curve gets its upward slope from the assumption that price equals the marginal cost of production in a competitive economy. With diminishing returns, less output requires less labor input and hence can be sold for less. Once we move off labor's marginal product curve and allow stockpiling, we may no longer have diminishing returns. That is, it may take more labor per unit of output to produce less than capacity output.

Recall the labor market diagram that we developed for the ILM model in Chapter 3 (Figures 3.7 and 3.8). We reproduce it here (Figure 4.2) along with a diagram of the goods markets. Similarly lettered points correspond.

Points A represent the long-run equilibrium. Businesspeople are paying labor its marginal product; there are no forecasting errors and the labor force is fully employed. Given the capital stock, the L_o workers employed produce Y_o. Y_o is full employment, capacity output.

Now consider the short-run effect of an *increase* in demand. We hypothesized that workers could make forecasting errors of the price level in the short run. As demand increases, prices and money wages are raised. Because the price increases are not completely foreseen, labor supply shifts right to S. Equilibrium in the labor market shifts from A to C. At point C more workers are employed, and their extra output is shown in Figure 4.3 as the horizontal distance from A to C, $Y_1 - Y_0$. An increase in demand leads to an increase in prices and employment, just as in the Neoclassical model. To the right of the long-run vertical economy supply curve, the short-run curve is upward sloping.

Now let us imagine a reduction in demand from the long-run equilibrium point A. In the last chapter we argued that if prices are inflexible, labor demand would be the vertical line D_2. D_2 represents the minimum amount of labor necessary to produce the reduced level of output Y_2. But we also noted that it may be profitable for firms to stockpile skilled labor, so that in the short run, labor demand may not shift all the way over to D_2, but instead to some intermediate point such as B. The question then is, what price would be charged while operating at the non-equilibrium point B? It may appear that we are involved here in a circularity, for we derived the vertical labor demand curve D_2 by *assuming* rigid prices. How can we now ask what the price level should be? The answer is that we are seeking a justification for that, heretofore unsupported, key assumption.

     Inflation and the Goods Market

Figure 4.2
The Labor Market According to the ILM Model

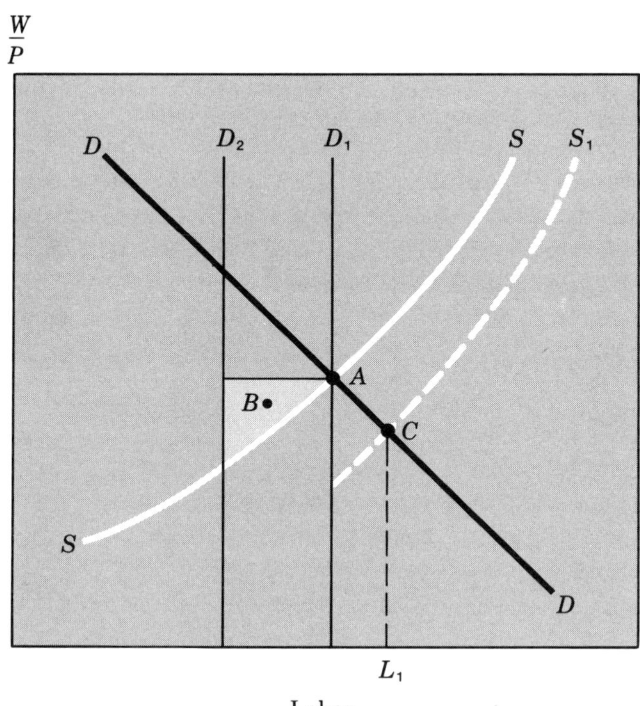

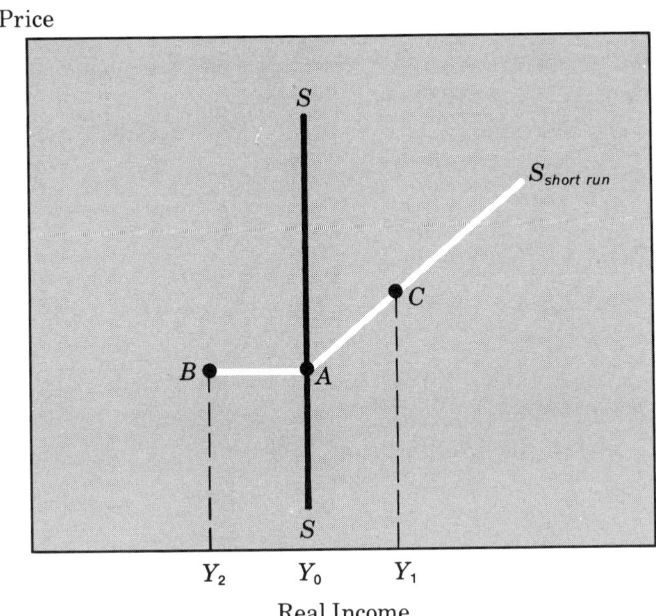

Price
S
$S_{short\ run}$
C
B
A
S
Y_2
Y_0
Y_1
Real Income

There are many theories as to why prices might be inflexible downward. The best known is derived from the markup pricing model. Most sectors of the U.S. economy are dominated by a fairly small number of large firms that set price and let demand determine the level of output, at least in the short run. The natural question then arises: What rule do these firms use in setting prices? One response is that they set prices so as to earn a target rate of return on capital when operating at the normal level. There is a markup over variable costs equal to required profits per unit of output. Mathematically the markup pricing model can be written

$$P = \frac{WL}{Q} + \frac{rK}{Q}$$

where:

$$
\begin{aligned}
P &= \text{price} \\
W &= \text{wage} \\
L &= \text{labor units} \\
Q &= \text{output} \\
r &= \text{desired profit rate on capital} \\
K &= \text{capital invested.}
\end{aligned}
$$

For simplicity we are assuming here that there are no raw material inputs. The relationship between price and output depends upon what happens to the labor output ratio, L/Q, and the capital output ratio, K/Q, as output varies. Under diminishing returns one expects both, or a weighted average of the two, to rise as output increases. But a temporary decline is different because both installed capital and skilled labor are fixed. The firm does not sell its machines or fire workers that are temporarily idle due to demand fluctuations which are expected to be of short duration. That implies that both K/Q and L/Q will rise as sales decline. A firm which follows the markup pricing rule and is desirous of maintaining a target return on capital will raise its prices as sales decline, and not reduce them. The businessperson is therefore forced to raise price, because capital costs must be spread over fewer units of output. The reader should note that this sort of pricing behavior is not generally consistent with profit-maximization, because it does not take into account the effects of price on the level of sales. A monopolist, maximizing profits, should find it advantageous to lower prices in the face of falling demand, if fixed capital and labor are significant.

Another variant of the markup pricing model says that price rigidity results from the high costs of changing price in response to every fluctuation in demand. The firm takes a long-run point of view. It sets price so as to earn the target rate of return when operating at normal output levels, but does not change that price in response to every change in sales. Such a strategy makes sense in terms of building long-run customer relations as well. In a world where search is costly, it is beneficial for both customers and firms to establish a long-term relationship, which eliminates the need for shopping for the best price or advertising for new customers. The attachments can be retained if the customer feels that the price charged is reasonable or fair. A logical candidate for such a fair price would be the price which covered full costs at some normal output level; this is the long-run markup pricing model.

As Okun puts it:[2]

> It [the firm] can justify cost-oriented price increases—a desire evident in the dedicated, if fuzzy, statements that firms issue, insisting that higher costs 'force' them to raise prices. No supplier can tell his customers: 'As a result of stronger demand, I am now in a position to capture a larger share of the surplus from our relationship.' In effect, the supplier firm represents itself to its customers as a kind of procurement agency operating under a brokerage arrangement. The markup onto costs becomes a reasonable way to set a 'fair' price for the services of the firm.

Summarizing, in the modern sector of the economy, where firms are price setters rather than price takers, there are several strong reasons to expect prices to be relatively insensitive to falling demand. Upward price pressure will come from short-run markup pricers, constant prices from firms with a longer time horizon. But there is also a more competitive sector in the economy. In that sector prices should more closely follow marginal costs, and marginal costs more clearly reflect the long-run marginal product curve of labor. In drawing the aggregate supply curve, one must decide how important each of these groups is. I have chosen a middle ground in drawing the supply curve of Figure 4.3. I have assumed that in the aggregate, the downward pressure on some

---

[2] Arthur Okun, "Inflation: Its Mechanics and Welfare Costs," *Brookings Papers on Economic Activity*, 2 (1975), p. 363.

prices is just offset by the upward pressure on others, with the result that the overall price level remains constant as overall demand declines. If I am right, this constancy will cover up relative price fluctuations in which prices in the competitive sector will fall relative to prices marked up during recessions.

The empirical evidence in support of downward price rigidity is, I think, quite strong. Many economists have investigated the effect of demand on price, although few have investigated downward rigidity per se. The general conclusion of these studies is that demand has at most a small positive effect on product price. Nordhaus, surveying work on the determinants of prices, finds "the inability to find a significant impact of demand . . . surprising."[3] Cagan says, "Empirical studies have long found that short run shifts in demand have small and often insignificant effects, and that, instead, costs play a dominant role."[4] Even in one of the few studies which found a significant link between demand and prices, the size of the effect was small. At least three fourths of any change in sales ends up as a change in output, with only one fourth leading to a change in prices.[5] Thus the econometric evidence suggests that short-run supply curves are indeed quite flat.

In short, if the ILM model is correct, what we have is a kink in the short-run supply curve of the economy at, or around, the normal capacity output level. The reader should remember that this representation is an abstraction. What we are saying is that the slope of the supply curve changes significantly around this normal capacity output level. It may seem strange and inelegant to apply a different model to expansions and contractions, as we did in justifying the kinked supply curve. Yet I think that is a superficial view. In a deeper sense, the difference between the expansion and contraction models recognizes the irreversibility of time in

---

[3] William Nordhaus, "Recent Developments in Price Dynamics," in O. Eckstein, ed., *The Econometrics of Price Determination* (Washington, D.C.: Board of Governors of Federal Reserve, 1972), p. 35. See also Otto Eckstein and David Wyss, "Industry Price Equations," in the same volume.

[4] Phillip Cagan, *The Hydra-Headed Monster* (Washington, D.C.: American Enterprise Institute, 1974).

[5] Robert J. Gordon, "The Impact of Aggregate Demand on Prices," *Brookings Papers on Economic Activity*, 3 (1975). See also Nordhaus's comments on Gordon's paper in the same issue.

economic processes. The simplest example of that is fixed capital. As the firm expands it acquires capital, but it doesn't divest itself of this capital when it contracts. Expansion and contraction are different. In expansion the problem is to select an optimal output and produce it at minimum cost. But in contraction the firm must confront the fixity of its capital and the skills of its labor force. It is not rational to simply throw those away, and therefore the firm does not necessarily maximize short-run profits or minimize short-run costs during contractions.

Goods Market Equilibrium

As in the labor market, *equilibrium* is defined as a point at which buyers are willing to buy exactly what producers are willing to produce. Since the supply and demand curves are the collection of all the output-price combinations satisfactory to buyers and sellers, the equilibrium we are looking for is the intersection of the two curves, a point at which supply equals demand. Because we have two supply curves, we can speak of a short-run equilibrium using the short-run supply curve, and a long-run equilibrium using the long-run curve.

To understand how price and output are determined over time, we have only to analyze how the demand and supply curves shift. For example, if we find that the aggregate short-run supply curve shifts upward over time, while the demand curve is fixed, we predict a period of rising prices and falling output. If the demand curve shifts upward, while the supply curve is fixed, we expect rising prices and rising output. We shall now put our analyses of the product and labor market together into a temporally interconnected or dynamic model of how prices and output move in response to a demand stimulus. This is what we will call the *inflationary process*.

Questions

1. Why is the aggregate supply curve upward sloping in both the Keynesian and expectations models? Under what conditions could it be flat or downward sloping?
2. There is a kink in the short-run supply curve in the ILM model. At what price and output level does it occur? Why?

3. Discuss why the aggregate demand curve is downward sloping. Why couldn't we derive the aggregate demand curve by simply summing up the demand curves of all individuals?

4. What is the difference between the short-run and the long-run supply curves?

Suggestions for Further Reading

Eckstein, Otto, and David Wyss, "Industry Price Equations," in Otto Eckstein, ed., *The Econometrics of Price Determination*. Washington, D.C.: Federal Reserve Board, 1972.

Gordon, Robert J., "The Impact of Aggregate Demand on Prices," *Brookings Papers on Economic Activity*, 3 (1975), 613–671.

Maccini, Louis J., "The Impact of Demand and Price Expectations on the Behavior of Prices," *American Economic Review* (March 1978), 134–145.

Means, Gardiner C., "The Administered Price Thesis Confirmed," *American Economic Review* (June 1972), 292–307.

Nordhaus, William D., "Recent Developments in Price Dynamics," in Otto Eckstein, ed., *The Econometrics of Price Determination*.

Okun, Arthur M., "Inflation: Its Mechanics and Welfare Costs," *Brookings Papers on Economic Activity*, 2 (1975), 351–390.

Chapter Five

A Description of the Inflationary Process

We now have a picture of how prices, wages, and output are determined period by period, and are ready to put these analyses together. It is useful to say a word at the outset about the method we are going to use. The method must be dynamic because inflation is a dynamic process. In this type of analysis, we are seeking a model which will determine a sequence of output and prices through time rather than the price or output level for a particular moment. This differs from the usual procedure in macroeconomics. Generally we study problems like the determination of income. This is an equilibrium analysis, for we derive a value for income or prices in equilibrium, where demand equals supply. By contrast, inflation analysis is a disequilibrium or dynamic analysis. It studies the process by which prices and other variables move over time, perhaps as the economy moves from one equilibrium to another.

In order to make dynamic analysis easier, economists have adopted a convention. They artificially break up time into periods and study the determination of prices (when studying inflation) during each period.

When they put the periods together, they have a price path. It is somewhat like making a movie by pasting together a set of still pictures.

While studying inflation we are going to make use of this period analysis, so our problem will be to understand how prices, output, and employment are determined during each period, and how the current period is influenced by the past and by expectations about the future. In our analysis the feedback mechanism, the link between periods, will be labor's reaction to previous forecasting errors. A key element in our theory will be the kinked short-run supply curve, which arises from the behavioral differences of the economy in booms and recessions. We use an exogenous shift in government expenditure as an example of an outside shock which generates an inflation. We will see how the economy makes a gradual adjustment in output and price to the change in demand conditions. Inflation is the name that we give to this dis-equilibrium adjustment process. As will be seen, the simple model we have been developing, coupled with a government determined to reduce the rate of inflation, together generate a price-output path for the economy remarkably like that produced by the United States since 1960. Thus actual experience tends to confirm the model.

The Expansionary Phase of an Inflation

The dynamic analysis we are going to present amounts to a prediction of shifts in the aggregate demand and supply curves over time. On the demand side we assume that shifts in the demand curve are determined outside our model; that they are exogenous to it. We concentrate on the supply side, where our model implies predictable shifts in the aggregate supply over time.

There are two reasons for shifts in supply. The first is techno-logical. Over time new machines are built, and the labor force becomes more skilled. This is what economists call technical change. All these factors make a given labor force more productive over time. Because the aggregate supply curve is derived by asking how much output the employed labor force can produce, technical change will be shifting this supply curve out over time.

The second reason why aggregate supply can shift is changes in expected prices by the labor force. In Chapter 3 we showed how a

Figure 5.1
Goods Market Equilibrium During Periods 1, 2, and 3

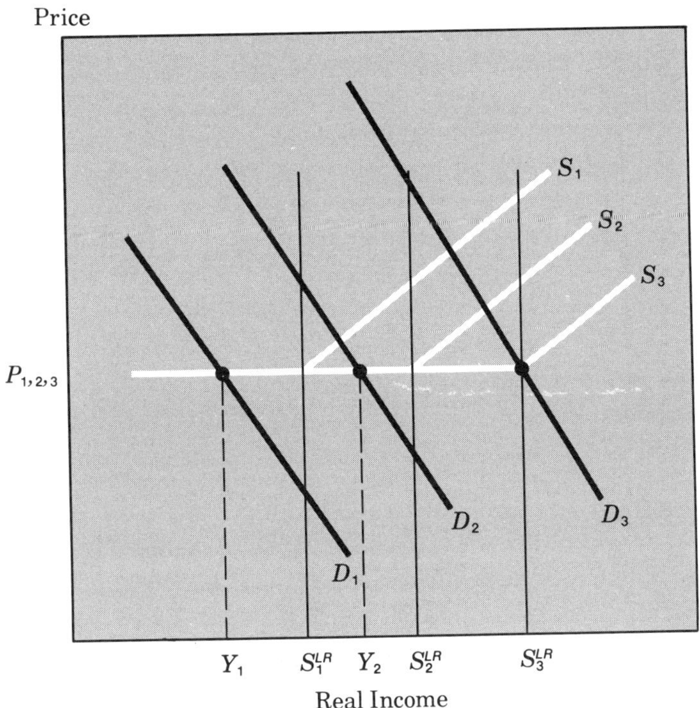

    A Description of the Inflationary Process

rise in the expected price level shifted the labor supply curve to the left. Translated to the goods market, a rise in expected prices shifts the aggregate supply curve of the economy to the left. By the same reasoning a fall in expected prices shifts the supply to the right. The reason is that the change in expectations changes the terms on which the unemployed can be hired.

Let us start our economy in a period of postinflationary recession with high unemployment and a negligible rate of inflation. In the first period the interaction of supply and demand in the goods market determines aggregate income and the price level. Why is unemployment in the recession abnormally high? It is high because demand reductions have shifted the economy onto the flat part of the kinked short-run supply curve. Perhaps the low level of demand stems from the attempt to stabilize a previous inflation. We might note here that the explanation of a Neoclassical economist for the high unemployment would be different. He or she would say that it results from an overforecast of inflation by labor, leading to wage demand inconsistent with the level of aggregate demand.

It may be useful to introduce a diagram of the economy to illustrate the process of change we are analyzing (Figure 5.1). Because we are going to follow the process over time, we must date our demand and our supply curves. The three vertical lines labeled S^{LR} are the long-run classical supply curves of Chapter 4. These curves show the output the economy can produce when machinery is operated at normal rates and when the labor market is in long-run equilibrium. Technical progress, capital formation, and increases in the labor force shift these curves to the right, in the United States, at about 2.4 percent per year. These long-run supply curves are a reference point for the analysis that follows, because each period's short-run supply curve, S_1, has its kink at the intersection with the same period's long-run curve. If the demand curve intersects short-run supply to the right of the long-run curve, the economy will be experiencing a boom; if the intersection is to the left, the economy is in a recession. Thus in period one, demand intersects the short-run supply curve at Y_1, less than capacity output for the economy in that year.

Suppose that the government decides to engage in new spending programs in period two. It may send men to the moon, build roads, enlarge subsidies or lower taxes. In the United States we engaged

in all of these demand-increasing activities during the early 1960s.
In Figure 5.1 the demand curve shifts outward in period two. As we
have portrayed it, the shift in demand is larger than the increase in
capacity but still not enough to reach full employment output.
Output expands from Y_1 to Y_2 and the price index stays constant at
P_1.

During period 3 the multiplier effects of the government program
continue to work themselves out. Businesspeople find that their
profits have risen and previously unemployed workers now have
jobs, so disposable income of both labor and management has risen
during period 2. Hence private consumption expenditures rise
during period 3. The demand curve shifts still further to the right.
Let us suppose that during this period the increase in demand is
just sufficient to intersect the period 3 short-run supply curve at
the long-run capacity level of the economy. The economy has now
fully recovered from the previous recession ($Y_3 = S_3^{LR}$). From now on
non-inflationery growth in output is possible only to the extent
that the long-run supply curve moves outward.

During period 4, suppose that the government is congratulating
itself on the success of its recovery program—for it has "gotten the
country moving again" without an increase in inflation—when it
is confronted with the necessity of increased spending. The most
obvious example might be a war, but any sudden jump in private
sector demand would have the same effect. Ideally the government
should raise taxes or reduce other spending programs of its own at
this point, but let us suppose that it does not. The result is another
rightward shift in aggregate demand (see Figure 5.2). But the
economy no longer has idle machines or idle workers to supply the
additional output being demanded by the government. Business
can increase output by hiring more labor, but the real product of
extra laborers is falling. To offset the resultant loss in real product
(MPP), business must either be able to pay lower nominal wages or
raise its own selling prices. It cannot hire workers at lower wages,
because no one is willing to work at a lower real wage than that
implied by the preceding year's nominal wage and price levels. So
prices rise. This enables business to increase output and employment. Remember that this works only as long as nominal wage
demands do not fully reflect the change in prices—that is, under
our assumption that labor does not perceive the change in prices.
What we see in period 4 is the start of an inflation. As the reader

can see from Figure 5.2, the shift in Demand to D_4 causes ouput to rise to Y_4. Now for the first time there is inflation. This is due to the fact that demand has increased faster than the capacity of the economy.

$$\frac{P_4}{P_3} > 1.$$

The position of the short-run supply curve in period 5 is somewhat complicated. If workers expect no further inflation during period 5, they will expect the actual price level of period 4 to continue during period 5. That being the case, the long-run equilibrium is at the price level P_4 where the short-run and long-run supply curves intersect (see Figure 5.2). Of course, actual prices need not remain at P_4. As always this will depend upon the level of aggregate demand as well as aggregate supply.

In period 5 the government is faced with a decision. Should it cut off the incipient boom by reduced spending, or should it bask in the optimism generated by high levels of employment and output after the previous years of stagnation and recession? Let us suppose that it goes the latter route and maintains its period 4 expenditure levels. Although government demand has leveled off, private sector spending increases, because of the delayed multiplier effects of the period 4 increase in government spending. This means that once again the aggregate demand curve shifts to the right.

Let us suppose that the increase in aggregate demand is greater than can be produced without a further rise in prices. Output rises to Y_5, prices to P_5. The economy is apparently in the middle of a demand-pull inflation. We would prefer to label this part of the inflationary process the expansion phase. It is characterized by rising prices, output, and employment. Typically it occurs at the beginning of an inflationary cycle. During the expansion phase of an inflation, prices are rising faster than anticipated. There is unexpected inflation. This is what causes boom conditions during expansions.

The Stabilization Phase

At some point during an inflation the government typically decides that it must take steps to limit further inflation. Usually this is done by contractionary monetary and fiscal policy, the aim of which is to shift the aggregate demand curve to the left. Contractionary macropolicy by the government which is intended

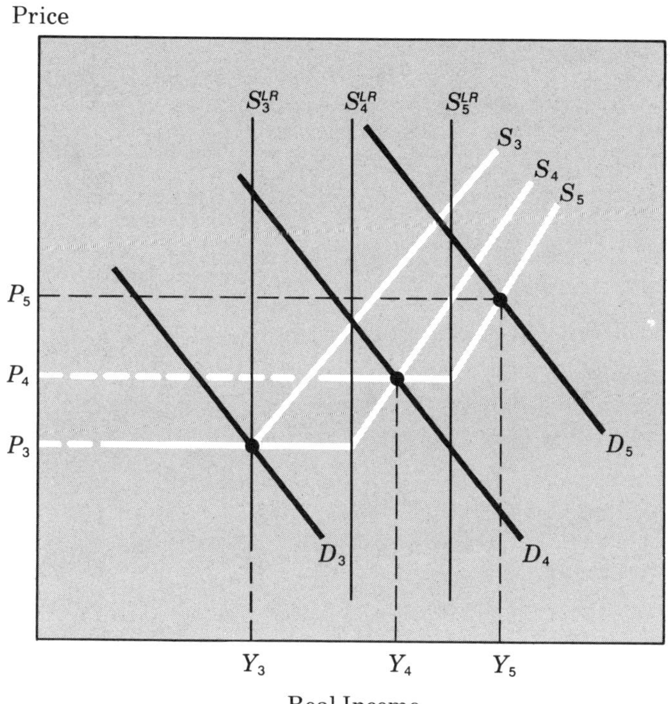

Price
S_3^{LR}
S_4^{LR}
S_5^{LR}
S_3
S_4
S_5
P_5
P_4
P_3
D_5
D_3
D_4
Y_3
Y_4
Y_5
Real Income

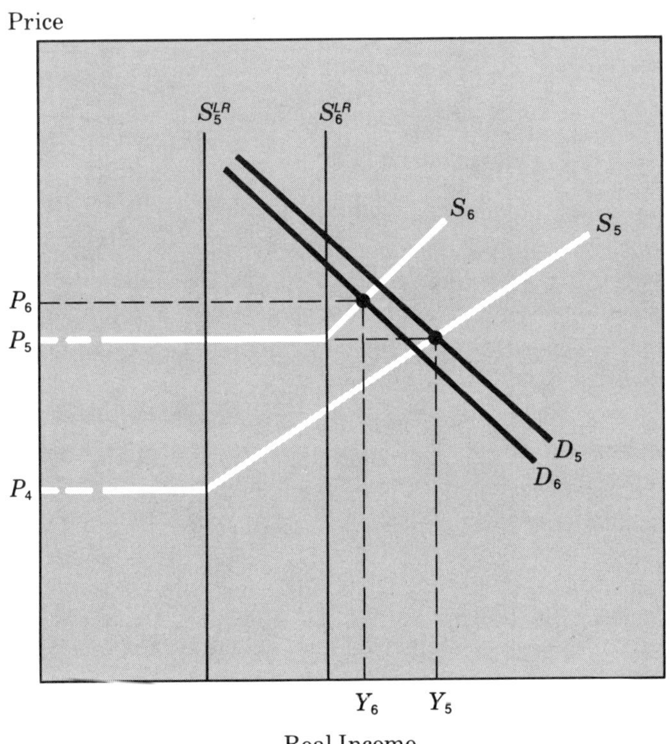

 Inflation and Unemployment

to stop or slow down an inflation is called *stabilization*. Thus we label the phase of an inflation during which the government is engaged in such policies the stabilization phase. As we will see, most of the macroeconomic policy controversies arise during this part of an inflation.

Let us suppose the government decision to stabilize takes place during period 6 of the inflationary process we have been analyzing. Because of the shift to contraction, the aggregate demand curve moves to the left of D_5. But this policy will not immediately bring inflation to a halt because supply conditions are still changing in an inflationary way. Consider Figure 5.3. For ease in comprehension, we have magnified the curve shifts so that we are able to see more clearly how the equilibrium point shifts between periods 5 and 6. In period 6 labor discovers that it again has underforecast the price level in period 5. As in period 4, let us again assume that labor continues to expect no further inflation—i.e., labor expects a continuation of period 5 prices in period 6. Labor demands an increase in wages to offset the price rise of the last year. This, of course, causes an upward shift in the short-run supply curve. By the definition of long-run equilibrium, S_6 intersects S_6^{LR} at P_5. Whether or not prices continue to rise during period 6 depends upon the relative size of the shifts in demand and short-run supply. As we have drawn it in Figure 5.3, the inflation continues, albeit at a slower rate, because the government is unwilling to reduce demand as fast as supply is falling.

We can see that if supply conditions were to remain unchanged $(S_6 = S_5)$, period 6 equilibrium would have lower output and prices. The inflation would be stopped. But because there was an unexpected inflation during period 5, it is unrealistic to suppose that the effective supply curve remains in its period 5 position. By experimenting with various hypothetical period 6 supply curves, the reader can see that as long as S_6 lies further to the left of S_5 than D_6 lies from D_5, prices continue to rise. Output falls regardless. What we are saying is that, if effective capacity in the economy falls faster than demand, there will be excess demand at the previous level, and prices must rise.

At the beginning of a stabilization it is highly likely that supply will be falling faster than demand. How far does the supply curve shift? Remember that the shift is caused by the rise in nominal wage demands by workers less the rate of technical progress. If last year's inflation was 4 percent and there is a 2 percent annual increase in productivity, labor will be asking for 6 percent higher wages, 4 percent to offset the inflation and 2 percent for technical change. In order to supply the same quantity of goods, the typical factory must raise its selling prices by 4 percent. In other words, the supply curve should be 4 percent higher at the previous year's output level. While this is not the same as the curve having shifted to the left by 4 percent, it will not be too far wrong to think of supply as shifting to the left each year at about the rate of the previous year's inflation.

The demand curve will probably be making much smaller shifts. Generally, stabilization programs are gradual and mean only that previous rates of growth in government spending are reduced. It is not likely that a government would knowingly reduce aggregate demand by 4 percent in response to a 4 percent inflation the previous year. The most likely stabilization sequence is a series of leftward shifts in supply greater than in demand, and therefore rising prices and falling output.

We have drawn the period 6 supply and demand curves to represent a gradual stabilization in which there is a small reduction in demand in relation to the reduction in capacity or supply. Prices continue to rise during the period, but now, for the first time, output falls. This rise in prices appears to be a result of the reduction in effective capacity due to wage demands. For this reason this phase of the inflation used to be labeled cost-push. Wages rise faster than prices, and output falls—all the classic symptoms of a cost-push inflation. But if our description of the process is accurate, the wage demands in period 6 were caused by the inflation in period 5, which was caused ultimately by the increase in government expenditures in period 4. In other words, the phase of an inflation when prices and wages are increasing and output is falling cannot really be separated and labeled. It is the stabilization phase of an inflationary process which was initiated by excess demand. In the new equilibrium, both prices and wages will have adjusted to the new conditions. But if we are right in our assumption that labor reacts to price changes with a lag, the adjustment in wages and prices is not simultaneous. Instead, there are two phases, the first when prices are increasing while labor is being fooled by inflation, and the second when prices and wages are both reacting. Typically in the first phase, output and employment are expanding, because the rise in nominal wages then occurring is taken by labor to be an equivalent rise in real wages. The extra production which occurs during that part of the process is in some sense involuntary. It would not have occurred had labor been fully aware of price trends. The second phase of the process is the correction of these mistaken price forecasts by labor and the elimination of involuntary overemployment and production. Wages and prices continue to rise and output falls. This is the stabilization phase, an integral and unavoidable part of the entire process which follows from erroneous price forecasts.

The reader should ask himself or herself what the adjustment to excess demand would be like if nominal wages reacted instantaneously to price changes. We have already seen that this would make it impossible to increase output through inflation. An economy might have an inflation, but there would be no boom in real output or employment. Rising prices would serve only to redistribute a constant amount of total goods among the various buyers in the economy. More germane to our point, if the wage and price adjustments were instantaneous and simultaneous, the entire price adjustment would occur immediately and there could be no talk of demand-pull or cost-push inflation. It is only in a world of imperfect foresight or, equivalently, sticky wages that this adjustment requires a number of periods and involves the kinds of feedbacks between inflation and wages that we have been describing.

One could say that imperfect foresight allows the economy to have its total inflation on the installment plan. As we know, the long-run economy supply curve is vertical. A shift outward in demand by the government will result in an increase in prices great enough to reduce private spending by the same amount as the multiplier times the new government spending program. Thus the total amount of inflation is constant. With imperfect foresight it is undergone over a number of periods instead of all at once, as it would be under perfect foresight. Employment and output temporarily exceed their long-run levels. Far from blaming labor for excessive wage demands during the stabilization phase, the public should be happy it did not have the inflation sooner.

The Effect of Expected Inflation
on the Adjustment Process

The inflationary cycle that we have just analyzed was one in which workers never learned to expect inflation. They demanded catch-up wage increases, but never an increase to cover inflation during the negotiating period itself. Judging by the experience of the last decade, the zero-expected inflation model is not a very reasonable portrayal of how labor behaves. Labor has learned that inflations usually continue and that it makes sense to build an inflation forecast into wage contracts. We now adapt our model for positive expected inflation and show the far-reaching effect that this change in behavior has for successful stabilization.

Let us return to our hypothetical economy. Recall that during period 6 the economy suffered its first decline in output, coupled with a deceleration in inflation. Suppose now that in period 7 labor begins to anticipate inflation. When that happens, nominal wage demands will rise to cover both the inflation of period 6 and the further inflation expected during period 7. This, of course, implies a larger reduction in effective capacity than before. Diagrammatically, the short-run supply curve shifts to the left by more than it did before (Figure 5.4).

Suppose that during period 7 workers expect a continuation of period 6 inflation. That means they expect prices to rise again in period 7 by as much as they did in period 6. What effect does this have on the short-run supply curve in period 7? This can be determined by recalling that the short-run curve S_7 intersects the long-run curve S_7^{LR} at the price level forecast by labor. That price level is P_7, the actual price level in period 6 inflated by the period 6 inflation rate. Had the labor force continued to forecast zero future inflation, S_7 would have intersected S_7^{LR} at the price level P_6. Thus the shift to positive expected inflation causes a much larger leftward shift in short-run supply in the economy. This has disagreeable implications for policymakers, as might be imagined.

The government is now faced with an unpleasant choice. If it continues with its stabilization program, there will be a large increase in unemployment and a deepening of the recession. If it allows demand to increase, the inflation will be even worse. If

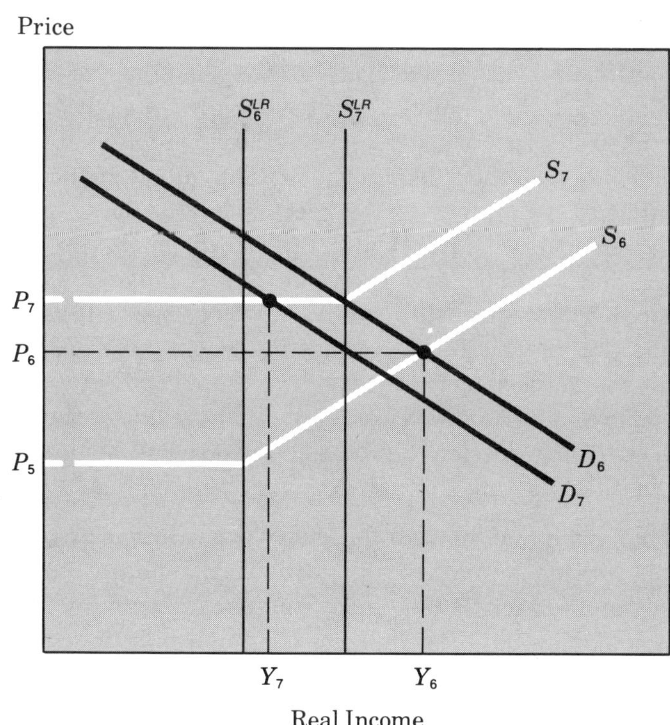
Price
S_6^{LR}
S_7^{LR}
S_7
S_6
P_7
P_6
P_5
D_6
D_7
Y_7
Y_6
Real Income

aggregate demand is reduced to D_7, output will fall to Y_7, which implies a very large increase in unemployment. For the first time, the economy enters a true recession in which there is involuntary unemployment in the sense that we used the term in Chapter 3, and in which output is below the capacity level (that is, $Y_7 < S_7^{LR}$).

What is equally distressing is that the inflation does not abate. It continues at the period 6 rate. As the reader can see by looking at Figure 5.4, this result follows technically from our drawing of the kinked short-run supply curve. If the curve is flat at less than full employment, then demand reduction cannot reduce the rate of inflation below the rate expected by the labor force. In the Friedman-Phelps Neoclassical world, the short-run supply curve was downward sloping. F-P would expect that demand reductions could help reduce the rate of inflation. We will return to this question in Chapter 7, because the whole theory of stabilization hinges on the shape of the short-run supply curve at less than full employment. Here we simply note that the flatter the curve is, the deeper the recession will be, and the less will be the reduction in the inflation rate through manipulating aggregate demand.

The switch to positive inflationary expectations by labor is a crucial turning point during the stabilization phase. So long as labor is simply reacting to previous actual inflation, it is possible to reach a new equilibrium price level in a relatively painless way. Involuntary overemployment is gradually eliminated as real wages approach their equilibrium level, but there is no involuntary underemployment.

Once expectations of future inflation are positive, it is no longer true that the total inflation in response to an initial increase in demand is constant, nor can price stability be reached without a period of involuntary unemployment. Involuntary overemployment exists during the expansion phase due to the artificial drop in the real wage at which labor is willing to work. But with positive expectations about future price changes, the actual real wage will be at the full employment level only if the expected rate of inflation materializes. During a stabilization program the aim of the government is precisely to reduce actual inflation below the expected level. Typically it does this by contractionary monetary and fiscal policy. If these policies are effective, there will be a period of high involuntary unemployment, whenever labor's expected rate of inflation is greater than that acceptable to government.

We need not continue our period analysis in such great detail. After the onset of positive inflationary expectations, the government has the choice of holding demand constant and incurring high unemployment, or ratifying those expectations by allowing demand to expand at the rate necessary to equalize actual and expected inflation. In that case employment and output stabilize at their long-run levels, but with a permanent inflation. This is probably what has occurred in several Latin American countries. Expectations about inflation have become so firmly positive that the cost of reducing them is a very long period of stagnation and above-normal unemployment. Rather than pay that cost, several Latin American governments have adjusted their financial and tax systems to a permanent inflation. It is not clear that this is an unwise policy decision.

When the government maintains a restrictive demand policy, there is a period during which prices continue to rise although there is also idle capacity and involuntary unemployment. We have drawn the short-run supply curve as flat, but eventually the pressure of the unemployed may moderate wage demands and idle capacity may induce firms to lower their prices. How long this process takes is still an open question. It depends upon how long it takes to drive expectations about inflation back to an acceptable level. As long as they are above that level, price stability cannot be achieved without a high cost in unemployment and reduced output. Our experience in recent years does not encourage much optimism on that score.

Comparison of the Hypothetical Inflation Process and Actual Inflations

The hypothetical sequence of employment, output, and price change we have described corresponds quite closely with recent U.S. experience. Arthur Okun describes the process by which the United States entered a serious inflation during the last half of the 1960s.[1] We came out of the 1950s with substantial

[1] Arthur M. Okun, *The Political Economy of Prosperity* (New York: W.W. Norton, 1970).

excess capacity and unemployment, which were the result of a long stabilization period after the Korean War. President John F. Kennedy was determined to get the country "moving again," and he proceeded to do this by increasing government expenditure and cutting personal income taxes. By 1964 or 1965 we were back at so-called full employment. At just that moment the United States became enmeshed in a costly war in Vietnam. We no longer had the excess capacity in men or machines to supply the extra output required by that conflict. For reasons that will be debated by the historians, there was no effective reduction in demand elsewhere until about 1968, when the tax surcharge went into effect. The result was the worst inflation since the Korean War. The hypothetical scenario we used to generate our inflationary process corresponds closely with this actual set of events.

One way to compare the theoretical and the actual results is to look at price and output in the goods market over time. Keep in mind that all we ever observe are intersections of supply and demand curves. We have an idea what the curves should look like, but we never observe them. Our theoretical analysis leads us to expect a certain sequence of supply curve shifts which imply that the actual intersection points will behave in a definite predictable way. By comparing our prediction with the actual event, we can test our theory of the inflationary process.

Figure 5.5 shows all the supply and demand curves that we have developed for the various periods described. The subscripts, as before, refer to the period. Since equilibrium in any period is the intersection of supply and demand, one finds it by looking at the intersection of supply and demand curves with the same numerical subscript. Each intersection is marked with a dot. From period 7 on, the demand curve is constant.

The process as we have described it traces a counterclockwise cyclic movement in real income. Starting from the initial recession, the economy has a period of expansion in output with no inflation. Then as demand continues to rise, there is a period of what used to be called demand-pull inflation. Output and prices are both increasing. We have called this phase of the inflation the expansionary phase. It includes periods 4 and 5. Eventually, demand stops rising fast enough to offset the leftward shifts in supply, and output begins to fall, even though prices continue to

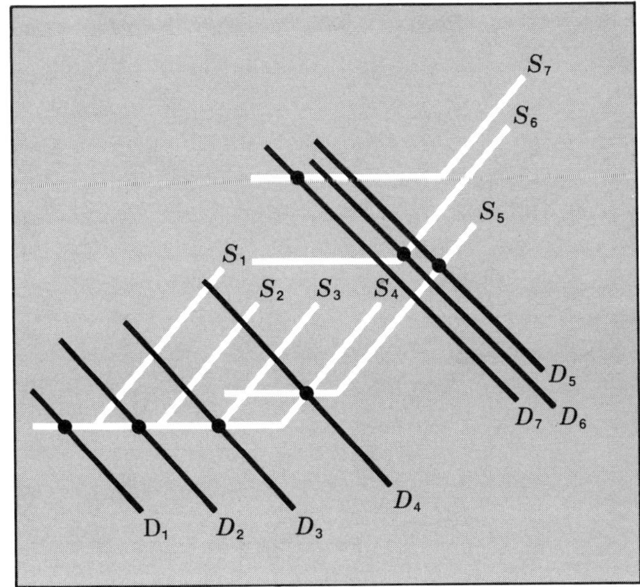

Price
Real Income
S_1
S_2
S_3
S_4
S_5
S_6
S_7
D_1
D_2
D_3
D_4
D_5
D_6
D_7

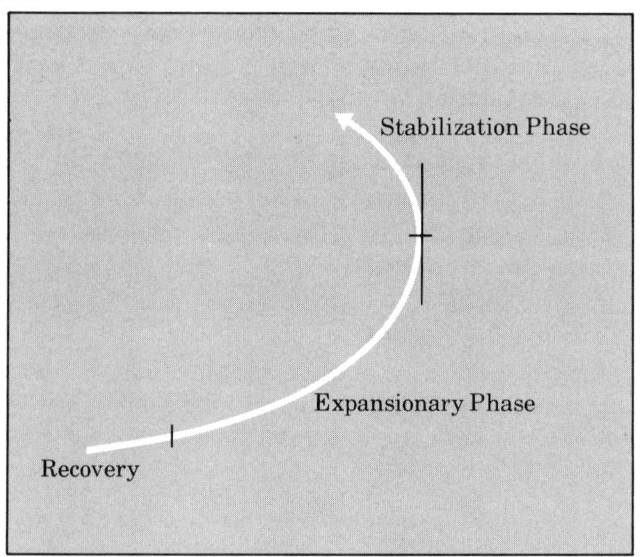
Price
Stabilization Phase
Expansionary Phase
Recovery
Real Income

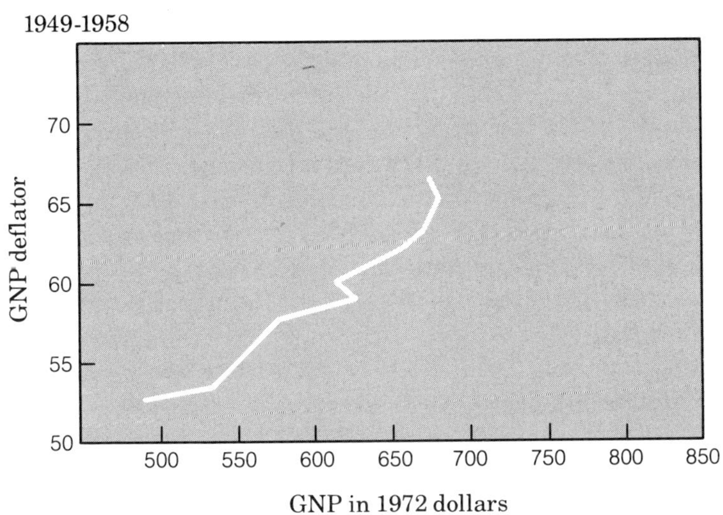

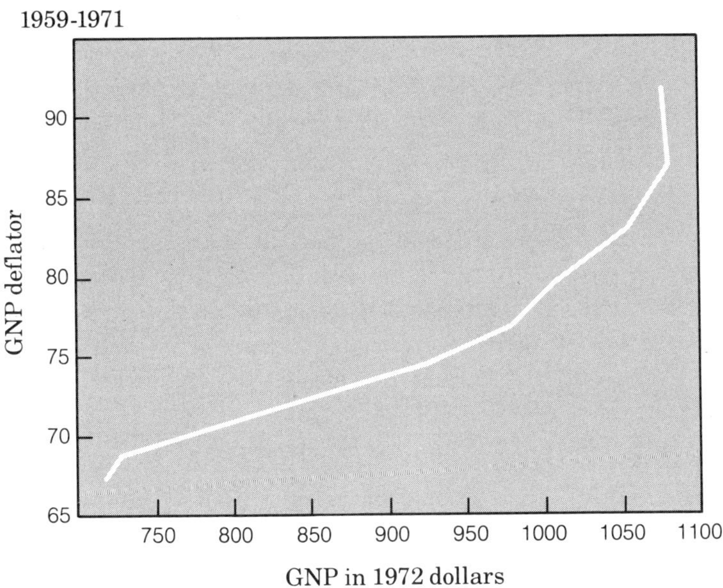

    A Description of the Inflationary Process

rise. Because demand is no longer rising, we have called this phase of the inflation the stabilization phase. It includes periods 6 and 7 in our diagram. Successive equilibrium points now move north-west on our diagram, instead of northeast.

Thus the typical inflation should move through the sequence of output-price combinations shown in Figure 5.6. Let us compare this with the actual U.S. experience of the 1950s and 1960s. In Figure 5.7 we plot real GNP against the GNP price index for the relevant years. As can be seen, the typical counterclockwise movement predicted by our model is confirmed for both inflations. The pattern is somewhat distorted by price controls during the Korean War, but one can view the late 1950s as the stabilization phase of the Korean War-World War inflations. Analysts and economists invented the term cost-push inflation to describe the period, but if one accepts our theory that stabilization and pre-ceding expansion cannot be separated, the late 1950s were the inevitable result of previous war-generated excess demand.

We have stopped our historical graph in 1971. That is because the subsequent period was interrupted by so many exogenous shocks, such as the oil embargo and the world crop failure as well as changes in macro policy, that it cannot be expected to conform to the neat inflationary cycle process pictured in Figure 5.6. For the period before 1971, the historical path of prices and output is extraordinarily close to the prediction of our theory.

Cost-Push and Demand-Pull Inflation

Economists attempted in the past to differentiate between cost-push and demand-pull inflations. Demand-pull in-flation is caused by an increase in demand relative to supply; more is demanded at each price, perhaps because of a war, an increase in the money supply, or new investment opportunities. Prices rise because there is excess demand at last year's prices, caused by the rightward shift of the aggregate demand curve.

Cost-push inflation comes from a leftward shift in the aggregate supply curve. The most obvious cause of such a shift is a demand for higher money wages by labor. We know that a rise in wages will force each employer to cut back output unless he can sell at higher prices. In the aggregate this implies a leftward shift in the short-run economy supply curve. This contraction in supply produces excess demand just as surely as an excessive rise in the money supply would, only this time it is because the effective capacity of the economy has fallen. Prices rise until the excess demand is eliminated.

It is not only labor demands that can produce these capacity reductions. An economy could depend heavily on imported inputs such as coal, oil, or steel. If the prices of imports rise, domestic business must charge higher prices. A nation can become technically less productive over time. Its fixed capital may wear out, its supplies of natural resources may be exhausted, or it may have a bad agricultural harvest. Each of these causes a leftward shift in supply, excess demand at the previous period's prices, and inflation. Such inflation is caused by a fall in supply instead of a rise in demand.

The term wage, or cost-push, inflation seems to have gone out of style, although it is being revived. The reason is that it is so very difficult to determine the cause of the rise in nominal wages which moves the short-run supply curve to the left. This rise is quite likely to be justified by previous price increases. Walter Reuther's comments on that subject are quoted here.

> The data reveal beyond all possibility of doubt that in each of the last three inflationary periods (including the current one), price increases preceded increases in labor costs. Moreover, the price increases were not necessitated by increases in other costs as indicated by the fact that, in each case, profits per unit of output were rising even before prices began to rise. The rises in unit labor costs began much later than the increases in prices—in the case of the current inflation, roughly 18 months later for manufacturing and later still for nonfinancial corporations.
>
> The increases in unit labor costs occurred primarily because of the workers' need to protect themselves and their families against erosion, resulting from *prior* price increases, of both their living standards and their share of the fruits of technological progress.
>
> In other words, the indisputable evidence makes it clear that inflation was triggered, in each case, by corporations and not by workers. In each case, the thesis expressed by the late General Motors President, C. E. Wilson, as long ago as 1952, was borne out. Mr. Wilson wrote:

"I contend that we should not say 'the *wage*-price spiral.'
We should say 'the *price*-wage spiral.' For it is not
primarily wages that push up prices. It is primarily prices
that *pull* up wages" (emphasis in original).[2]

A glance at Figures 5.8 and 5.9 bears Reuther out. The rise in labor
costs has come after the rise in prices. Our interpretation would be
that it is a delayed reaction by labor to unexpected inflation during
the early stages of a boom.

According to our view of the inflationary process, there is a predictable sequence of shifts in the demand and supply curves during
the typical inflation. First the demand curve shifts out, generally
because of an increase in government expenditure. We call this the
expansionary phase. Labor's reaction to the initial price increase is
a delayed demand for wage adjustments. This causes a leftward
shift in the short-run supply curve and the rising wages and prices,
which have been labeled cost-push inflation. But if we are correct,
this cost-push phase is related to or caused by the preceding
demand-pull phase. It makes little sense to speak of rising wages
as the cause of the rise in prices. We prefer to think of this stage of
an inflation as the stabilization phase.

The Trade-off between Output and Inflation

One of our principal contentions in this book is that
the expansionary and stabilization phases of an inflation are related, that they are part of a single process. It follows from this that
there is no permanent trade-off between output and inflation.
Proponents of an expansionary policy used to say that one could
buy extra output and employment for a little bit of inflation. But
they were looking at the expansionary phase only, and were
forgetting the inevitable stabilization. You could say that they
were taking the short-run point of view. In the short run, as we
have seen, higher prices do bring more output and employment,
but only because the price increases are not anticipated. During
the ensuing stabilization phase, all the extra output is eliminated

---

[2] Letter to economists from Walter Reuther, dated December 18,
1969. Reprinted by permission of United Automobile Workers.

Figure 5.8
Prices and Labor Costs

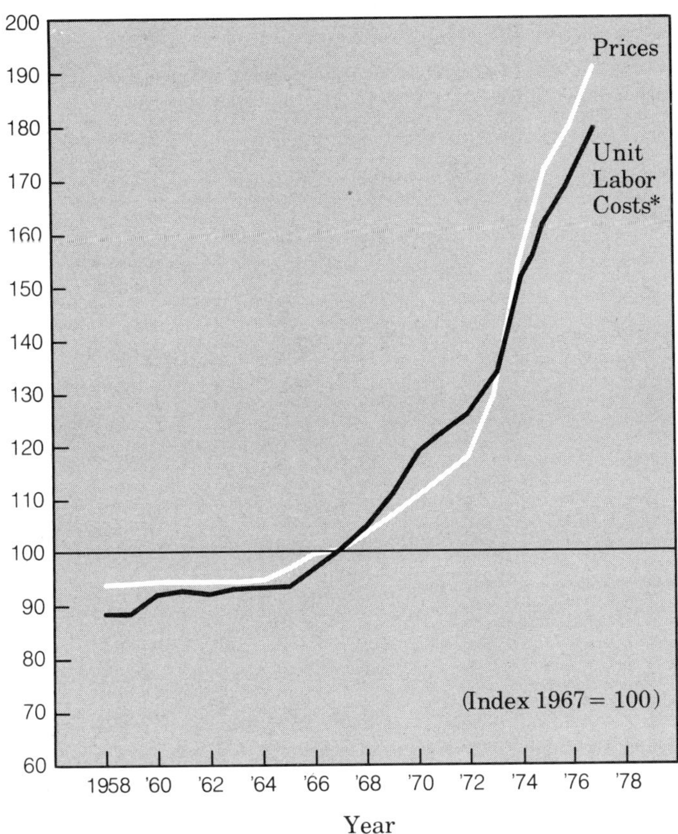

Wholesale Price for Manufactured Goods   (Index 1967 = 100)
Compensation of employees per unit of non-farm business output.
Source: *Survey of Current Business*. U.S. Department of
Commerce.

Figure 5.9
Prices and Profits Before Taxes

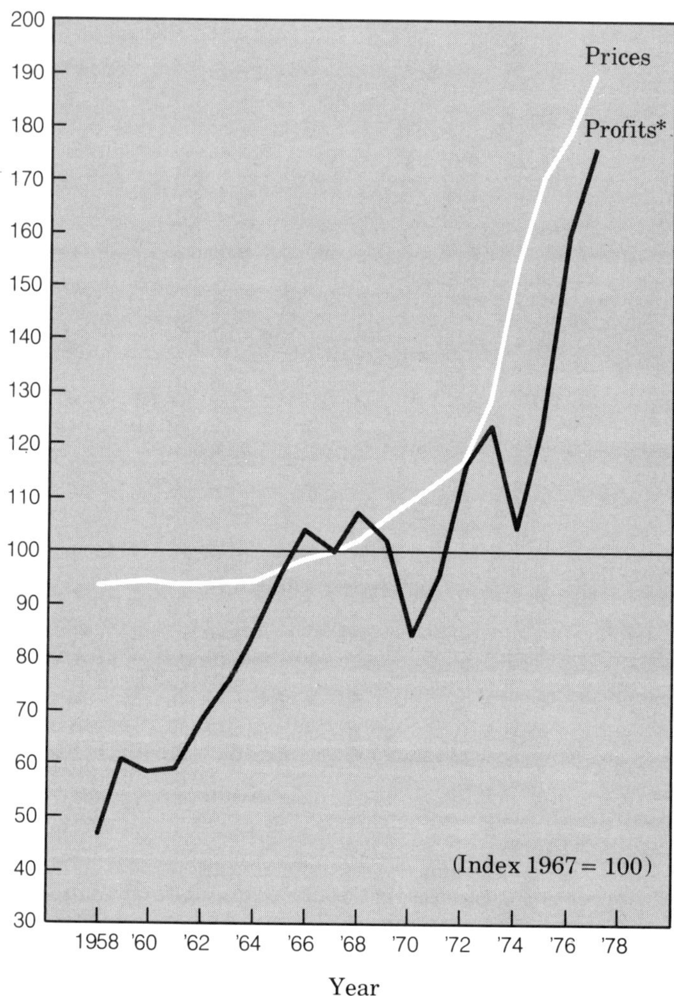

Wholesale Price for Manufactured Goods   (Index 1967 = 100)
*Corporate profits before taxes with inventory valuation adjustment.

Source: *Survey of Current Business*, U.S. Department of Commerce.

as labor adjusts to new price levels. At best the inflation brings a temporary increase in output and employment.

In the long run, the capacity of the economy is determined by the productivity of the labor force. Capacity is fixed by technical factors such as the capital stock, resource endowment, and education level of the population. It is not influenced by prices. As we have seen, the long-run aggregate supply curve is vertical and shifts outward over time. In the short run the economy can get off the long-run curve, because wage adjustments to inflation are not instantaneous, meaning that, temporarily, rising prices will raise output. Eventually, however, the economy must return to its long-run curve, meaning that all the extra output above that produced by changes in productivity is eliminated. If throughout the entire inflation labor never acts as if it expected inflation, the situation can be depicted as in Figure 5.10a. High prices result in a temporary income bulge, but the permanent result is simply higher prices.

The situation changes fundamentally if expectations by labor adjust to the inflation. When labor expects future price increases and adjusts nominal wages accordingly, price stability can be achieved only by a period during which output and employment fall below their long-run rates. In other words, with positive expected inflation during the inflationary process, there must be a period during which the economy is to the left of the long-run supply curve. Then we have the S-shaped movement around the long-run supply curve shown in Figure 5.10b. During the expansion phase there is a temporary northeasterly movement (that is, above-normal output with unexpected rising prices). This is followed by a fall to less than normal output with still higher prices. With positive expected inflation, we no longer get just a temporary bulge in output. Now the extra output is balanced by a later shortfall. The trade-off is not between inflation and output, but between output now and output later. Higher than normal output during the expansionary phase is counterbalanced by lower than normal output during the stabilization phase.

As Milton Friedman has put it:

> "There is always a temporary trade-off between inflation and unemployment; there is no permanent trade-off. The temporary trade-off comes not from inflation per se, but

     A Description of the Inflationary Process

(a) Zero Expected Inflation

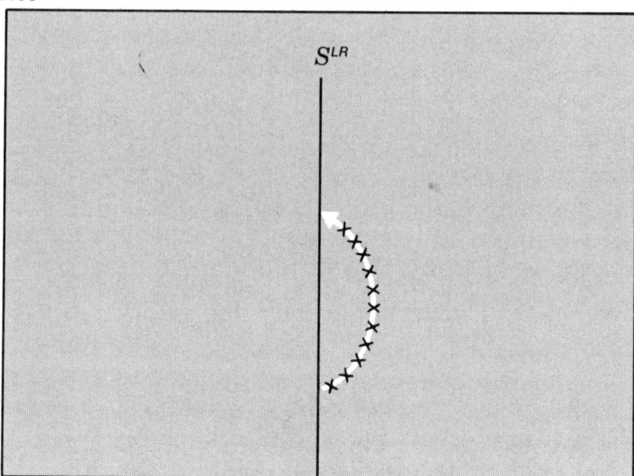

(b) Positive Expected Inflation

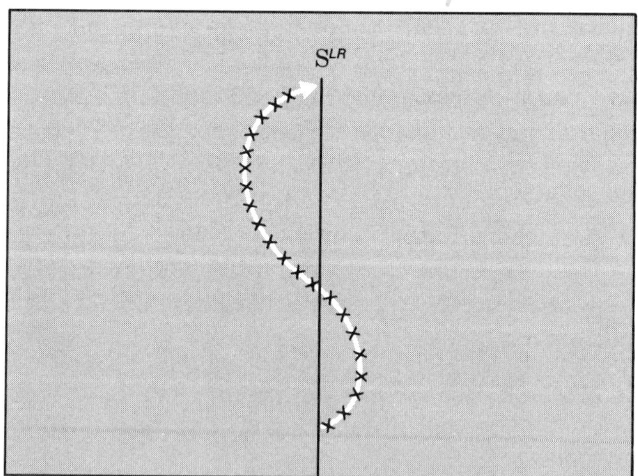

 Inflation and Unemployment

from unanticipated inflation, which generally means from a rising rate of inflation. The widespread belief that there is a permanent trade-off is a sophisticated version of the confusion between 'high' and 'rising' that we all recognize in simpler forms. A rising rate of inflation may reduce unemployment, a high rate will not."[3]

If the kinked supply curve represents supply conditions in the economy, the inflation-output trade-off is even less attractive than Friedman implies. If prices are inflexible downward for the reasons advanced in Chapters 3 and 4, inflation does not fall below the expected rate, even with high unemployment. The inflationary cycle has the form of the extended S shape of Figure 5.11, as long as the government tries to get back to a lower rate of inflation.

The Neoclassical view underlying Figure 5.10b suggests that contractionary macropolicy will eventually be able to reduce the inflation rate to its original level. That is, the economy after some delay will move in a northeasterly direction in Figure 5.10b. But the ILM model of Figure 5.11 is far less optimistic about the downward flexibility of prices. It asserts that inflation rates are insensitive to contractionary stabilization policy, and predicts that the economy will move north rather than northeast in the diagram, even at high rates of unemployment. This is why ILM economists do not advocate orthodox stabilization. It is not that they like inflation; just that they do not think that stabilization will cure it.

For a Neoclassical economist like Milton Friedman, the most likely inflation-output trade-off is the more output now/less later variety, assuming that when the cycle is over, inflation rates return to their original level. For the ILM economist, the trade-off is seen as more output now, less later plus a permanently higher inflation rate, which is due to the inability to bring it back to its original level except by an unacceptably severe recession.

Our experience in the United States with inflation has been a bitter one. If expectations had been slow to adapt to inflation, we perhaps could have raised output temporarily by an inflationary policy. But it is clear that labor is thoroughly aware of inflation.

---

[3] Milton Friedman, "The Role of Monetary Policy," *American Economic Review* (March 1968).

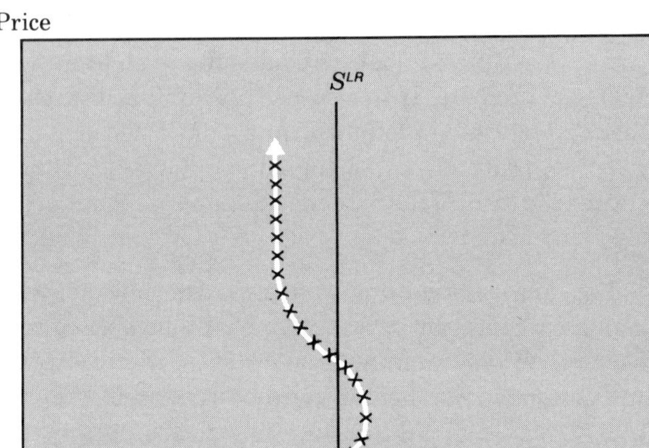
Price
S^LR
Real Income

Contracts being signed reflect strongly positive expected inflation. Thus the inflation-output trade-off in our economy is going to be of either the Neoclassical or ILM variety. In return for temporary booms we will pay with either a recession, or a recession plus a permanently higher inflation rate. In either case, inflation is not a very appealing policy for increasing GNP or employment.

Questions

1. Define cost-push inflation and demand-pull inflation. Is it useful to distinguish between the two?
2. What are the different possible inflation-output trade-offs? Why isn't there ever a permanent trade-off between inflation and output according to Friedman?
3. How might the cyclic pattern of output and prices be different in economies with slow and fast adjustments of expectations to inflation?
4. What would happen to the cycles we have described if all contracts had cost-of-living escalators?
5. If the government wishes to eliminate inflation in an economy in which the labor force has come to expect inflation, then there will be a period of recession. Do you agree or disagree with this statement? Why?

Suggestions for Further Reading

Friedman, Milton, "A Monetary Theory of Nominal Income," *Journal of Political Economy* (March–April 1971), 323–337.

Okun, Arthur M., *The Political Economy of Prosperity*. New York: W. W. Norton, 1970.

Parkin, J. Michael, and G. Zis, eds., *Inflation in the World Economy*. Manchester: Manchester University Press, 1976.

Samuelson, Paul, and Robert M. Solow, "Analytical Aspects of Anti-Inflation Policy," *American Economic Review* (May 1960), 177–194.

Weintraub, Sidney, *Capitalism's Inflation and Unemployment Crisis*. Reading, Mass.: Addison-Wesley, 1978.

Chapter Six
The Phillips Curve

Up to the last few years, it appeared to be an empirical fact that, when rates of unemployment were high, the rates of change of prices and wages were low, and vice versa. This suggested a relationship or trade-off between unemployment and inflation which prompted an enormous amount of research and debate into the exact nature of the trade-off. Professor A. W. Phillips, one of the earliest investigators, plotted actual unemployment rates against wage changes for Great Britain from 1861 to 1957, and noticed that over each cycle the resulting points traced out a rounded L-shaped curve. This same relationship, now known as the Phillips curve, has been confirmed for the United States and extended to price changes as well as wage changes.

Figure 6.1 summarizes U.S. experience. Up to the 1970s a reasonably stable and close-fitting relationship between unemployment and inflation rates could be observed. The existence of the curve seemed to give the economy the choice between operating with low employment and low inflation rates or high employment and inflation. There seemed to be a trade-off between inflation and unemployment after all. A political debate raged over what point on the Phillips curve should be chosen as a target for policymakers.

Friedman and Phelps emphatically contested this interpretation of the historical record. They argued that the Phillips curve was a natural result of labor's short-run forecasting errors. Formally they showed that to each different rate of expected inflation there corresponds one short-run L-shaped Phillips curve. The reason why the curves seem to have been stable in the past is that periods of high inflation used to be followed by stabilizations before price expectations could fully adjust. In this chapter, we will examine the F-P argument and show that it is a logical extension of the labor market analysis of Chapter 3. We will then show how the contrasting views of F-P and the ILM theorists are reflected in a disagreement over the shape of the short-run Phillips curve when unemployment rates are above normal.

The Phillips Curve as a Result of Erroneous Price Forecasts

In Chapter 3 we were concerned with the determination of equilibrium employment and real wage levels. Now our attention is focused on unemployment, the other side of the employment coin. The U.S. Department of Labor defines as unemployed someone who is in the labor force, and who is seeking work, but is not working. In terms of the labor market diagram of Chapter 3 (Figure 6.2), unemployment is the difference between total employment and the labor force, or L_f-L_e.

Recall now the F-P model of the labor market previously discussed. According to F-P, workers must forecast prices as they make their nominal wage demands. When those price forecasts are wrong, what we called the short-run supply curve of labor diverges from the long-run curve, causing both employment and unemployment to change. That discussion was summarized in Figure 3.5 and in the following rules: whenever prices are lower than workers expect them to be, the short-run supply curve lies to the left of the long-run curve; whenever prices are higher, it lies to the right. Since unemployment is determined by the intersection of the demand curve with a short-run labor supply curve, this implies that whenever prices are higher than expected, unemployment is lower than normal and vice versa.

   Inflation and Unemployment

Figure 6.1
The Phillips Curve

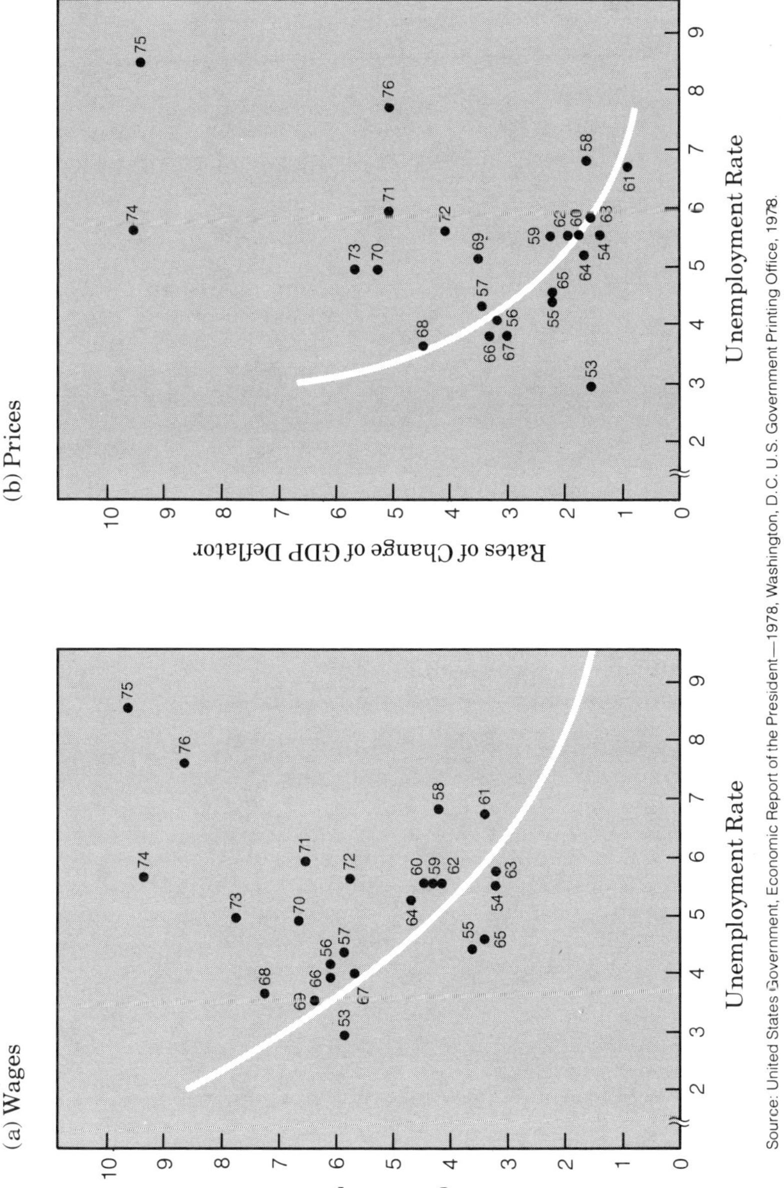

Source: United States Government, Economic Report of the President—1978, Washington, D.C. U.S. Government Printing Office, 1978.

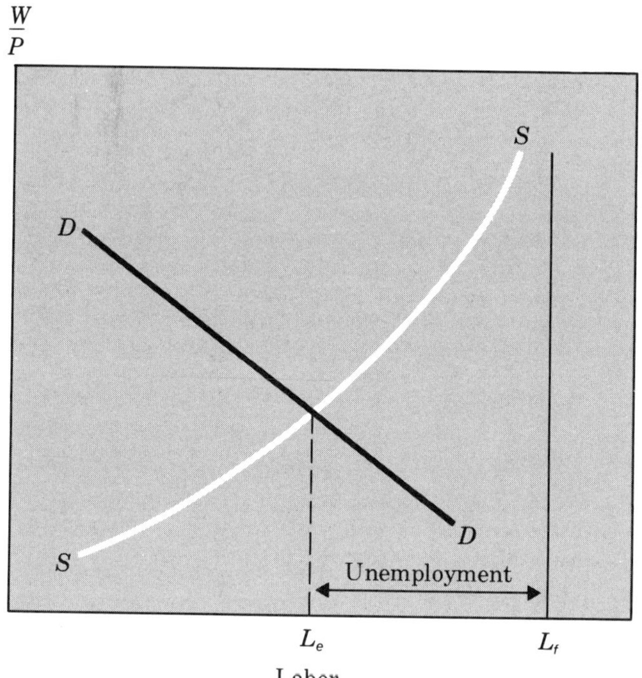
W
P
S
D
D
S
Unemployment
L_e
L_f
Labor

Let us translate this argument from price *levels* into rates of inflation. The actual rate of inflation can be written: $\dfrac{P_t^a - P_{t-1}^a}{P_{t-1}^a}$

where P_t^a means the actual price index in year t. The expected inflation rate is $\dfrac{P_t^e - P_{t-1}^a}{P_{t-1}^a}$ where P_t^e is the expected price level in year t. Since the actual price level of the past period, $t-1$, is known, whenever the actual price level in year t is greater than people expected it to be $(P_t^a > P_t^e)$, the actual rate of inflation during year t is also higher than people expected it to be.

$$\text{Formally:} \qquad \underset{\text{Actual Inflation}}{} \qquad \underset{\text{Expected Inflation}}{}$$

$$P_t^a > P_t^e \implies \frac{P_t^a - P_{t-1}^a}{P_t^a - 1} \; > \; \frac{P_t^e - P_t^a\,1}{P_t^a - 1}$$

To summarize: the F-P analysis of Chapter 3 yields the following predictions about unemployment and actual inflation rates:

Inflation higher than expected→Unemployment lower than normal

Inflation lower than expected→Unemployment higher than normal

Inflation equal to expected ⟶ Unemployment equal to normal

We now want to show that there is a short-run Phillips curve corresponding to each different level of expected inflation. To do that we must translate the analysis from Chapter 3 into inflation and unemployment rates. In that chapter we showed that there is a different short-run supply curve for each actual price level, holding expected prices constant. This can be translated immediately into inflation rates. Suppose that the labor force expects the rate of inflation to be 4 percent. That is $\dfrac{P_t^e - P_{t-1}^a}{P_{t-1}^a}$ = 4 percent.

Now perform a mental experiment. Vary the actual rate of inflation and, using the labor market diagram, find the resulting level of unemployment. As a base reference point, suppose the actual inflation rate is 4 percent. This is equivalent to saying that actual and expected prices are equal. There are no forecast errors and the short- and long-run labor supply curves coincide. Unemployment is at U_0, the normal or frictional level for the economy (see Figure 6.3). What if prices rise faster than 4 percent? If the actual infla-

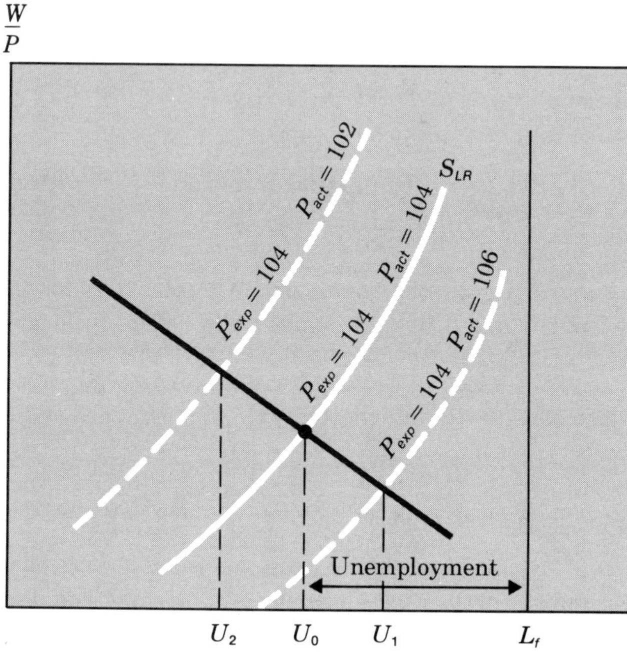
$\frac{W}{P}$
$P_{exp} = 104$
$P_{act} = 102$
$P_{exp} = 104$
$P_{act} = 104$
S_{LR}
$P_{exp} = 104$
$P_{act} = 106$
$P_{exp} = 104$
Unemployment
U_2
U_0
U_1
L_f
Labor

tion rate is 6 percent, for example, actual exceed expected prices. As we already know, if $P_a > P_e$, the short-run labor supply curve lies to the right of S_{LR}. Unemployment drops to U_1. At inflation rates lower than 4 percent, the opposite happens; unemployment rises above U^0—in the case of 2 percent inflation, to U_2 as shown in Figure 6.3. If we now transfer these points to a diagram of inflation and unemployment, we quite clearly are tracing out a Phillips curve relationshi (see figure 6.4). High inflation rates are associated with low unemployment rates, exactly what the P curve asserts.

A further implication of the F-P theory is that there is a different Phillips curve for each different level of expected inflation. This is easy to see. Suppose that labor expects 6 percent inflation instead of 4 percent. Then the short- and long-run labor supply curves coincide at an actual inflation rate of 6 percent instead of 4 percent. Unemployment will be U_0 when prices rise by 6 percent. Similarly, to reach the unemployment U_1, inflation rates would have to rise to 8 percent, because it is unexpected inflation that matters. Thus the 6 percent expected inflation Phillips curve is the dashed line in Figure 6.4. In general there is a different SR Phillips curve for each level of expected inflation, and the higher the level, the higher the curve. Each curve intersects the normal unemployment level U_0 where the actual inflation rate equals the expected rate for which the curve is drawn. We will call these curves short-run Phillips curves, for they show unemployment when actual and expected prices are unequal, which is analogus to the short-run labor supply curves of Chapter 3.

If there is a short-run Phillips curve for every level of expected inflation, the short-run curve says nothing about the possibility of a trade-off between inflation and unemployment. For one must expect labor to react to unexpected inflation by adjusting its rate of inflation upward. Thus, whenever the economy moves to the left up a short-run curve, it will tend to move vertically above the curve to higher curves as expectations adjust.

But the reader may protest, how can we say that the inflation-unemployment trade-off is not possible when historically the economy has actually moved out of a short-run Phillips curve? Suppose that you are a government economist, and you have found

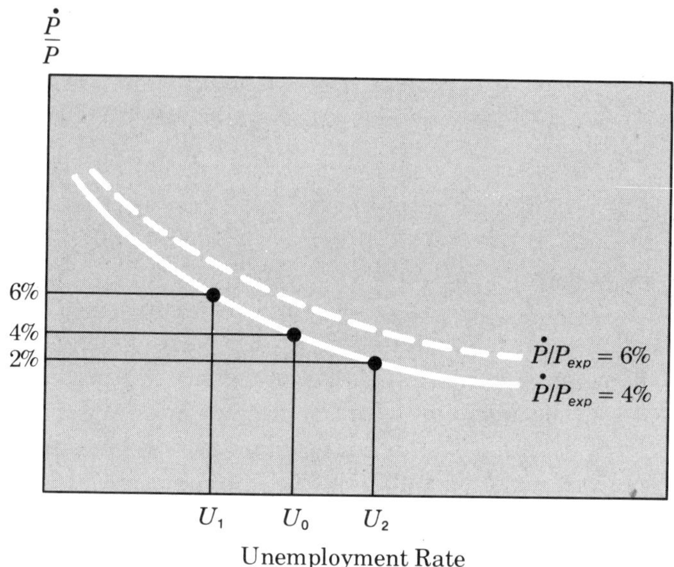
$\dfrac{\dot{P}}{P}$
6%
4%
2%
$\dot{P}/P_{exp} = 6\%$
$\dot{P}/P_{exp} = 4\%$
U_1
U_0
U_2
Unemployment Rate

a stable Phillips curve relation which indicates that the economy
has the following alternatives:

Unemployment (rate)	Change in Wages (rate)	Inflation (rate)
3%	3%	2%
4	2	0
5	1	−2

The 2 percent increase in real wages which occurs at 4 percent
unemployment is the result of increases in technical efficiency of
labor over time, owing to additions to the capital stock. Now
suppose the economy has actually moved from the 4 percent unemployment and stable price combination to the 3 percent unemployment with 2 percent inflation on several different previous
occasions. Would you not be tempted to present the two positions as
alternatives and argue that you could reduce unemployment by 1
percent at the cost of 2 percent inflation?

The government may view 2 percent inflation as a cheap price to
pay for a 1 percent reduction in unemployment, and proceed to
adopt expansionary fiscal policy to achieve the 2 percent inflation.
In period 1, nominal wages rise by 3 percent instead of the custom-
ary 2 percent. Prices also rise, although this is unexpected by
labor. Labor thinks that real wages have risen by 3 percent instead
of 2 percent, while business realizes that wages have risen 1
percent rather than 2 percent. The result is that employment and
output rise and unemployment falls. The government has reached
point A on the short-run Phillips curve. But unfortunately for
government, this is not the end of the story. In period 2, labor
reacts to the unexpected 2 percent inflation. Unemployment dropped in period 1, because labor thought that it was receiving a 1
percent larger than normal increase in its real wage. But in fact its
real wage rose by only 1 percent. To make up for this unexpected
loss, labor will therefore demand its usual 2 percent nominal wage
boost plus 2 percent for the unexpected inflation in period 1 plus a
further increase to offset whatever inflation it has learned to
expect. In order to hold unemployment at the 3 percent level, the
government finds that nominal wages must rise by more than 3
percent. But business cannot maintain the high employment level
unless the actual real wage stays at the period 1 level. This means

that inflation has to be greater than 2 percent. The government has to allow the inflation to accelerate in order to maintain the desired 3 percent employment rate. The trade-off seems to be evaporating as the economy moves to point B on a new Phillips curve, (Figure 6.5).

As soon as labor begins to expect future inflation and to demand wage increases to make up not only for past price changes but also for future ones, the rate of wage and price change required to maintain the 3 percent level of unemployment accelerates. As the history of unexpected inflation lengthens, this adaptation of expectations is bound to occur. Thus the government finds itself pursuing an unviable policy. Instead of having brought a 1 percent reduction in unemployment with 2 percent inflation, it has put the economy into an ever-worsening inflation for as long as it attempts to maintain the 3 percent unemployment level. This is because the 3 percent rate of unemployment is not at an equilibrium level. The economy achieves it in the short run only because of differences between what labor perceives the real wage to be and what it actually is. Each year, as labor adjusts to previous forecasting errors, greater and greater inflation is required just to maintain the same employment. The economy has to run harder and harder just to stand still.

Our analysis implies that it is not possible for the economy to stay permanently at any point on the short-run Phillips curve except at the long-run natural rate of unemployment. When the government tries to reach any other point and stay at that point, there is a gradually accelerating upward movement above the short-run curve. Here, then, is the answer to the puzzle of why the Phillips curve does not represent viable alternative states of the economy, even though the economy is generally on the curve. The curve is traced during the normal boom-recession inflationary cycle. Expansion historically has always been followed by stabilization. The cycle has reversed the upward adjustment of expectations, so that the economy has remained, more or less, on one curve. You could say, therefore, that the short-run curve is observable for actual economies exactly because it has never been used as the basis for policymaking. When a government attempts to move an economy out a short-run curve away from the normal unemployment level, there is a gradual (or perhaps not so gradual) upward movement of

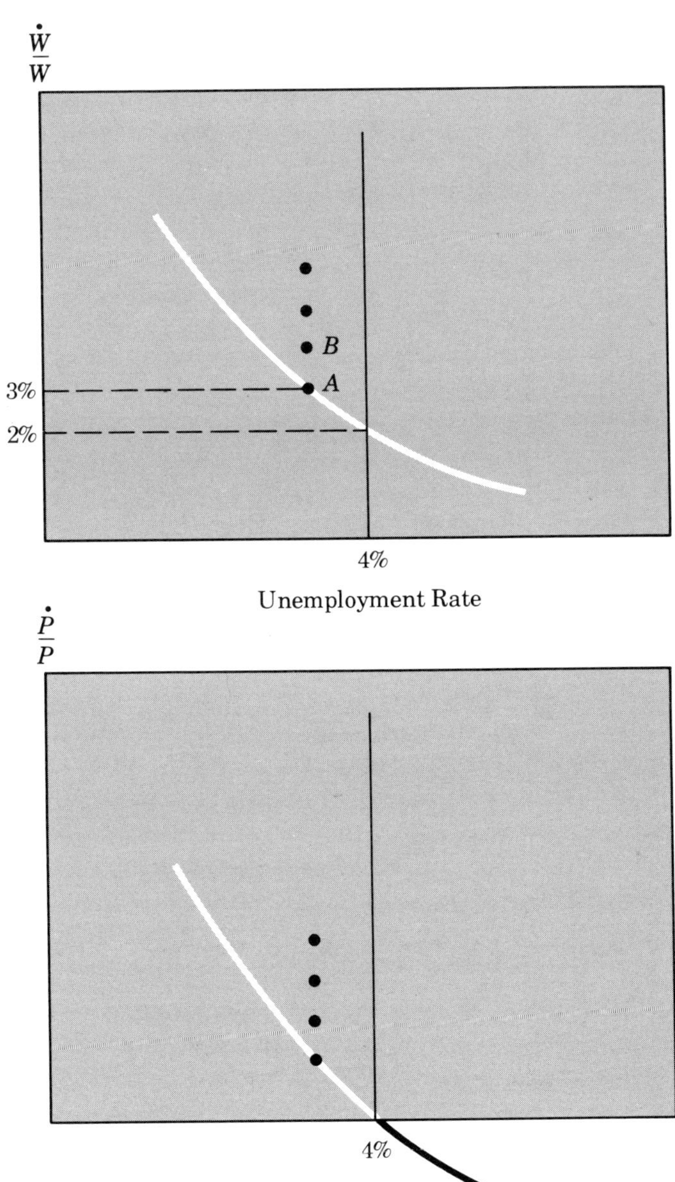

   The Phillips Curve

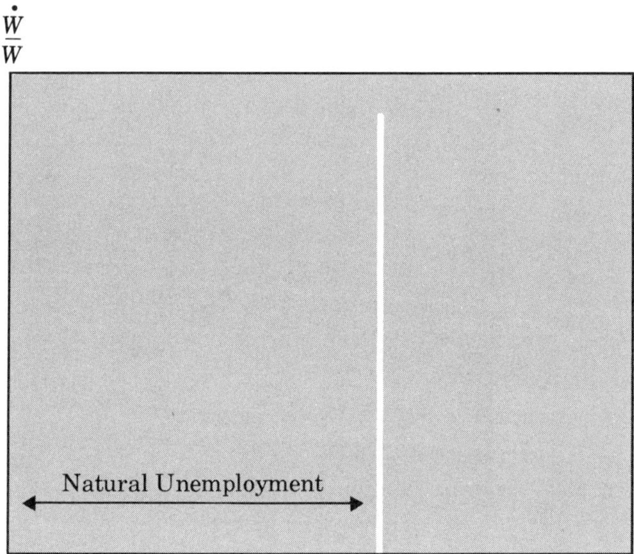
$\dfrac{\dot{W}}{W}$
Natural Unemployment
Unemployment Rate

the whole curve as the economy adjusts to unexpected inflation. Under such a policy one would not observe the short-run curve. One cannot use the observed Phillips curve as an indicator of the trade-off between inflation and unemployment.

Short-Run versus Long-Run Phillips Curves

In the goods market analysis, we saw that there was a big difference between the short run and the long run. This same difference shows up in the Phillips curve. Remember, we found that price increases could increase output in the short run. By our reasoning, this was because the price increase enabled business to increase nominal wages while still allowing real wages to fall. Because the inflation was unexpected, this situation induced higher than equilibrium labor supply and labor demand, a happy but temporary state of affairs. This is exactly what the Phillips curve says: wage increases reduce unemployment. But if the output-inflation trade-off was short run, temporary, so should the Phillips curve trade-off between wage boosts and unemployment be short run. They are merely different views of the same process.

Is there a long-run Phillips curve, and if so, what does it look like? Such a curve would tell us the relation between long-run equilibrium unemployment and wage changes, when there is no unexpected inflation. When inflation is fully forecast, no price change by itself can increase employment, because the change is immediately offset by an equal increase in nominal wages. In the long run, the only possible equilibrium in the labor market is the intersection of labor demand and labor supply curves. This determines employment and the real wage. At that real wage a certain additional number of people are seeking work. These are a revolving group of people who have been called frictionally unemployed. We do not expect this unemployment to drop to zero in long-run equilibrium, which is why Friedman called it the "natural" rate of unemployment.

Wage increases by themselves would increase the number of workers willing to work, but businesspeople are not willing to pay the higher wages unless they are offset by price increases. But if they are offset by price increases, no additional workers are willing to work. In the long run, only one level of unemployment is possible. By the term *natural unemployment*, we do not mean that this number is fixed and inevitable. Increasing information about job vacancies, retraining programs, and so on, would tend to lower unemployment. But at any point in time, with given labor market conditions, what we have on the Phillips curve diagram is a vertical line at the natural level of unemployment (see Figure 6.6).

The F-P analysis of the Phillips curve was in close agreement with U.S. experience during the 1960s. At that time, the natural or long-run equilibrium unemployment rate was thought to be 4 percent. The economy was approaching full employment by that definition around 1965, as can be seen in Figure 6.1. In subsequent years, as the increased volume of military expenditures continued to generate demand, inflation began to accelerate. From 1965 through 1967 there seemed to be a trade-off between inflation and unemployment. Inflation rose from 1.7 percent to 2.9 percent in return for a reduction in unemployment from 4.5 percent to 3.8 percent. But the economy could not remain with that trade-off. Just as F-P predicted, subsequent reductions in unemployment during 1968 and 1969 were accompanied by a steady acceleration in the inflation rate. The government was forced to abandon its 3.5 percent unemployment rate and turn to stabilization.

F-P were never particularly clear on the shape of the short-run Phillips curve at higher than normal unemployment rates, nor on the path an economy might be expected to follow during stabilization. So let us stop and consider the predictions of the theory about stabilizations.

Stabilization Paths

Consider first an economy in which there is no adjustment of expectations. In such an economy, the expansion phase of an inflation is the leftward movement up a particular short-run Phillips curve from *A* to *B*, and the stabilization phase retraces the route back down the curve to its intersection with the long-run curve from *B* to *A* (see Figure 6.7).

When there is an adjustment of expectations in response to unexpected inflation, either of two different inflationary cycles is possible. As the economy moves up a short-run curve, there is a gradual shift to higher and higher curves. This means that one

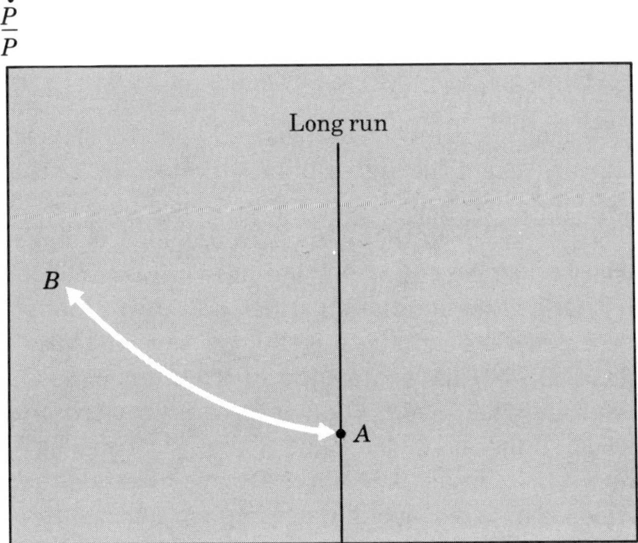

    The Phillips Curve

possible outcome for the economy is a return to the long-run curve at a permanently higher rate of inflation (Figure 6.8). Note here that the economy has a temporary boom which is counterbalanced by a permanently higher inflation rate. Note also that it is possible for the economy to move northeast in the Phillips curve diagram. All that is required is an increase in expected inflation greater than the increase in actual inflation. That causes a decline in unexpected inflation even though the actual inflation rate may still be rising.

The second stabilization path occurs when the government is unwilling to accept the higher inflation rate at point B. How can the rate of inflation be brought back to its original level? How can the economy return to the point A from which it started the inflationary cycle? According to F-P, this requires a reduction in labor's expectations about inflation, which can only be brought about by a period when the actual is less than the expected inflation. That, of course, also means greater than normal unemployment. During the phase when expectations are being revised downward, the economy must be to the right of the long-run Phillips curve, in range C of Figure 6.9. Why? Because during the adjustment period, labor is acting on the assumption that prices will rise more than they actually do, and is therefore demanding too high a real wage. Gradually, as actual inflation remains below expected, the economy moves back down to curve one, as shown by the dotted lines in Figure 6.9, and then returns to point A to complete the cycle.

Let us see how the ILM model can be translated into the Phillips curve framework and the implications for stabilization. Recall the two key behavioral assumptions of the ILM model. They are price rigidity and labor stockpiling in the face of insufficient aggregate demand. In such an economy, suppose that the government causes a recession in an attempt to bring down the rate of inflation. As demand falls below the level that would provide full employment at the current price level, what happens? According to F-P, prices fall and the real wage rises due to erroneous price forecasts by labor. It is the rising real wage which causes a rise in unemployment. Not so, say the ILM economists. Prices, or rates of inflation, are not reduced, so output falls. Unemployment gradually rises as marginal workers are released. If firms stockpile labor, new hiring stops. Over time, as new workers enter the labor force, the unemployment rate gradually rises.

Figure 6.8
Inflationary Cycle with Adjustment in Expectations

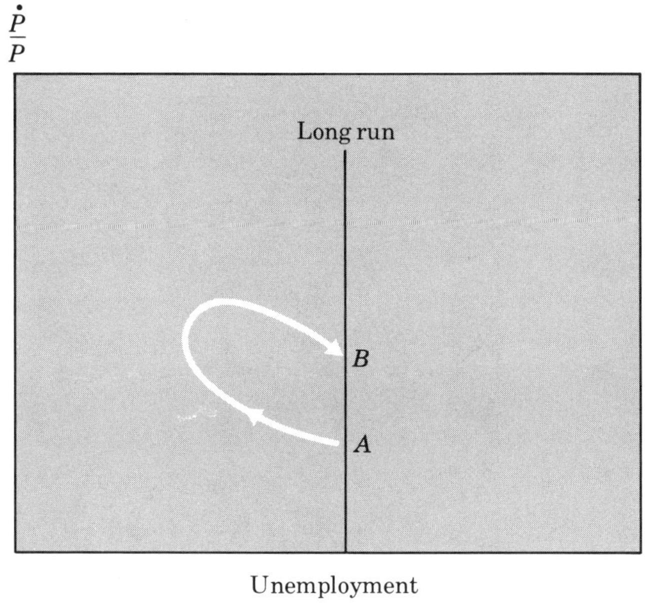

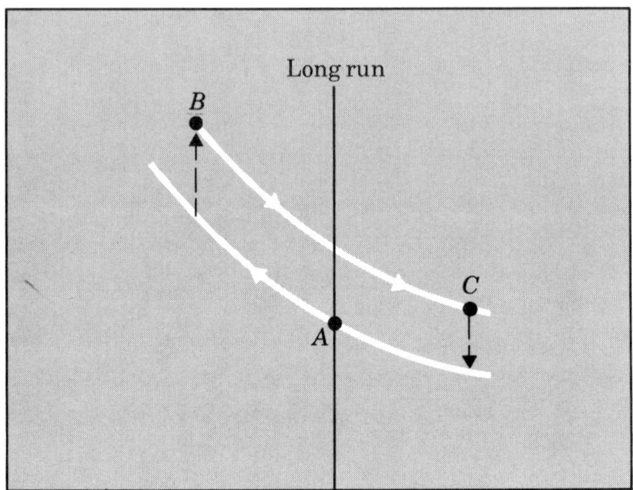
Long run
B
C
A
Unemployment

Translated into Phillips curve terms, the ILM stabilization scenario implies that the short-run Phillips curve has a kink at the full employment level, being flat at higher than normal unemployment rates. This kink is analogous to the kink in the ILM short-run aggregate supply curve discussed in Chapter 4. It occurs at the intersection of the short-run and long-run Phillips curves where actual and expected inflation rates are equal. Basically the kink stems from the assumptions of price rigidity (see Figure 6.10). Presumably there is a whole family of such kinked short-run Phillips curves, each corresponding to a different level of expected inflation.

Now consider an inflationary cycle according to the ILM model. The initial movement from A in a clockwise loop to B is not different from the F-P scenario. The differences become apparent at B only if stabilization continues in an effort to get back to point A. For instead of moving southeast from B, as F-P predict, the economy may move straight east (from B to C). Because prices are sticky downward in response to falling demand, the rate of inflation remains constant. Unemployment rises, but the forces drawing down the inflation rate are weak or nonexistent. Markup pricing in the presence of labor stockpiling and idle capacity are the chief factors making prices sticky downward. Furthermore, if inflation rates do not fall, expectations about inflation cannot be dropping either. That eliminates one source of downward pressure on nominal wages. The only other hope, the unemployed labor force, is not likely to put effective pressure on the wage rate of the employed either. That is partly because firms are not hiring, and partly because firms are reluctant to exchange workers with firm-specific skills for new workers, even if those new workers offer to work for less. The economy may then move out from point B to point C, but the forces that Friedman and Phelps expected would help the economy move back to point A—expectations adjustment, declining marginal cost, and falling rates of wage inflation—may be so weak that the economy comes to rest at C, a thoroughly unsatisfactory situation from everyone's point of view. Inflation is higher than acceptable to the government stabilizers, and unemployment is higher than normal.

We will return to the difficult problems of stabilization in Chapters 8 and 9, but first we think a discussion of the effect of inflation and stabilization on the distribution of income would be instructive.

Figure 6.10
The Short-run Phillips Curve
According to the ILM Model

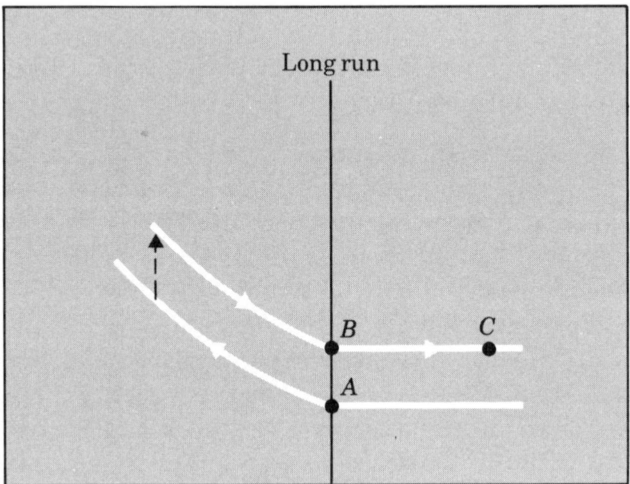

 Inflation and Unemployment

Questions

1. How might the Phillips curve traced by an economy in which there is a fast adjustment of expectations to inflation differ from the curve traced by an economy with slowly adapting expectations?
2. If, in the long run, there is no trade-off between inflation and unemployment, then in order to reduce the long-run unemployment level we would want to undertake policies designed to shift the long-run Phillips curve to the left. What policies would you suggest for accomplishing this goal?
3. Attempt to derive a Phillips curve, using the aggregate demand-aggregate supply analysis of the previous chapters.
4. "If, in the past, the government had used the Phillips curve relation as a guide to policy formulation, we would never have observed such a relation." What does this statement mean?
5. Explain what was meant by the phrase "inflation on the installment plan."
6. Is it possible to have rising inflation and rising unemployment at the same time? Explain in easily understood terms why this is or is not possible.
7. The ILM Phillips curve has a kink. At what inflation and unemployment rates does it occur? Why?

Suggestions for Further Reading

Brechling, Frank P., "Wage Inflation and the Structure of Regional Unemployment," *Journal of Money, Credit and Banking* (February 1973), 355–379.

Brunner, Karl, and Allen Meltzer, eds., *The Phillips Curve and Labor Markets*. Amsterdam: North-Holland Publishing Co., 1976.

Hansen, Bent, "Excess Demand, Unemployment, Vacancies and Wages," *Quarterly Journal of Economics* (February 1970), 1–24.

Holt, Charles C., and Martin H. David, "The Concept of Job Vacancies in a Dynamic Theory of the Labor Market," in *The Measurement and Interpretation of Job Vacancies*, New York: NBER Conference Report, 1966.

Lipsey, Richard, "The Relation between Unemployment and the Rate of Change of Money Wage Rates in the United Kingdom, 1862–1957: A Further Analysis," *Economica* (February 1960), 1–31.

Perry, George, *Unemployment, Money Wage Rates and Inflation*. Cambridge, Mass.: MIT Press, 1966.

Phelps, Edmund S., *et al.*, eds., *Microeconomic Foundations of Employment and Inflation Theory*. New York: Norton, 1970 (especially papers by Phelps, Holt, Lucas and Rapping, and Mortenson).

Phillips, A. W., "The Relation between Unemployment and the Rate of Change of Money Wage Rates in the United Kingdom, 1862–1957," *Economica* (November 1958), 283–299.

Tobin, James, "Inflation and Unemployment," *American Economic Review* (March 1972), 1–18.

Wachter, Michael L., "The Changing Cyclical Responsiveness of Wage Inflation," *Brookings Papers on Economic Activity*, 1 (1976), 115–169.

Chapter Seven

Changes in the Distribution of Income over an Inflationary Cycle

Prices, wages, profits and employment are all changing over an inflationary cycle. In this panorama of movement in relative and absolute prices and incomes, are there systematic changes in the distribution of income predicted by our various labor market theories? It is the purpose of this chapter to explore that question.

All of our theories suggest that the level of aggregate demand should have an important influence on the distribution of income among various groups. To focus this discussion let us divide up the population into four groups: the nonworking poor, the working poor or marginal labor force, the "mainline" labor force, and the owners of capital. What we are calling the "mainline" labor force is the vast array of skilled and unionized labor, lower level management and white collar bureaucrats. According to the ILM viewpoint, the employment of this group is relatively impervious to the economic cycle because of the skills it possesses. The marginal labor force is composed of unskilled workers, new entrants and other disadvantaged groups. This is the group which is the first to lose its jobs when aggregate demand turns down. What happens to the distribution of income between these four groups over the inflationary cycle?

The Nonworking Poor

By definition, the nonworking poor are outside the labor force, and are thus immune to the influence of the labor market. Their income is made up of transfers, such as welfare payments, pensions and social security. Rising prices could harm the nonworking poor, relatively or even absolutely if the money value of the transfers they receive is not adjusted upward to offset inflation and to keep up with growth in aggregate real income.

How have transfers fared relative to inflation and the overall level of real disposable income? A recent study shows that disposable income and transfer payments have by and large grown together in the postwar period.[1] Thus the expectation that inflation might harm the poor who live on fixed pensions, or welfare payments, is not borne out by the record. Indeed, as we shall see below, there has been a small but significant increase in welfare payments both in real terms and as a fraction of GNP during the 1970s.

The Working Poor

According to the ILM theories, the level of aggregate demand should have an extremely powerful effect on the relative and absolute income levels of the working poor. This is because of the extreme sensitivity of their employment prospects to labor market conditions. As we have already seen, under labor stockpiling, the mainline labor force is insulated from the full effects of recessions. Not so the marginal labor force. It is likely to lose its jobs during recessions, and to face job rationing as well. Conversely, during booms, jobs are easier to find for unskilled labor; family members may enter the labor force to supplement family incomes, and the wage differential narrows for skilled labor. On all these grounds, one should therefore expect the working poor to gain during booms and to bear the brunt of stabilization and recession.

[1] R. G. Hollister and J. L. Palmer, "The Impact of Inflation on the Poor," University of Wisconsin, Institute for Research on Poverty, Discussion Paper #40, 1969.

Unfortunately there is no generally agreed-upon definition of the marginal labor force and hence no easy way to test this prediction of the ILM theory. However, consider the cyclical behavior of unemployment rates for two particular groups, teenagers and blacks, which must contain a high proportion of the marginal labor force. In Figure 7.1 we show the relationship between the particular unemployment rates for these two groups and the national unemployment rate. One can perform a regression or fit a line to the scatter of points in Figure 7.1. This line tells us how group-specific unemployment moves with the national rate. For example, our regressions say that a change of one percentage point in the national unemployment rate changes black unemployment by 1.6 percentage points and teenage unemployment by 1.7 percent. That means that the unemployment rate of blacks or teenagers rises much more than proportionally during recessions and falls more than proportionally in booms. Thus it is painfully obvious from Figure 7.1 that the burden of recession is not equitably shared across the labor force. The employment prospects of blacks and teenagers are far more sensitive than the overall labor force to demand conditions.

Mainline Labor Force and Profits

We have seen that the marginal labor force gains much from expansions, irrespective of inflation. What about the other two groups in the economic pyramid, the mainline labor force and the owners of capital? As in so many other areas, the F-P and ILM models answer this question differently. The expectations model predicts that the mainline labor force has a gain in real wages and probably in income share during contractions, and a loss during expansion. The ILM model predicts the opposite. Both models agree that profits should be procyclical.

To understand these predictions it is useful to reintroduce the basic diagram of the labor market (Figure 7.2a and b). Figure 7.2a shows the Neoclassical version of the labor market during a contraction. We now want to use the diagram to show real wages, and profits. Note that the area under the labor demand curve *OGAB* is equal to total income at long-run equilibrium, and *OGDC* is total income during a contraction. The reason the area under the demand curve is equal to total income is that the demand curve

     Changes in the Distribution of Income

shows the marginal product of different quantities of labor. Therefore if one accumulates the marginal product of successive increments of labor, up to the number actually employed, one must have the total product of the economy. Now consider the labor and profit share of total product. Looking first at long-run equilibrium, since the real wage is height OF, the wage bill is the rectangle $OFAB$. Definitionally, profits equal the difference between total product and wages—the triangle FGA.

Consider now what happens to wages and profits during a contraction. Recall that the short-run labor supply curve shifts leftward during contraction because of an overforecast of inflation. Contractionary equilibrium is at D. At that point the real wage rises to OE, the wage bill is the rectangle $OEDC$ and profits shrink to the triangle EGD. Two unambiguous predictions of the theory, therefore, are a rise in real wages of those who remain employed and a fall in profits. Whether the share of profits in total income rises or falls depends on the shape of the demand curve.

Consider now the same contraction from the ILM viewpoint (Figure 7.2b). The long-run equilibrium of the two models is identical. However, during a contraction, the labor market is not in equilibrium. Product price rigidity, labor stockpiling and resistance to wage cutting lead to a short-run contractionary solution at some point like H in the shaded area of Figure 7.2b. Real wages fall to OE, the wage bill falls to $OEHC$ and profits fall to $EGKJ$ minus $JHCL$. Thus the burden of a contraction is borne by all parties. Some labor is stockpiled, but suffers a decline in real wages. Profits are hurt by the decline in productivity resulting from stockpiling. Total product is only $OLKG$, but stockpiled labor is paid $JHCL$ out of profits. As a consequence, if the ILM model is correct, the labor share of total income should surely rise during contractions. Note however that the position of H depends on the relative influences of unemployed workers on the wage, and of the forces leading to an expansion of output. If a contraction is protracted, one might expect the real wage to drift downward and stockpiled labor to be released. This could turn the profit share around. During a long contraction profits might first decline and then subsequently increase.

We have no way to separate the mainline and the marginal labor force, and so, no test which completely differentiates between the

     Inflation and Unemployment

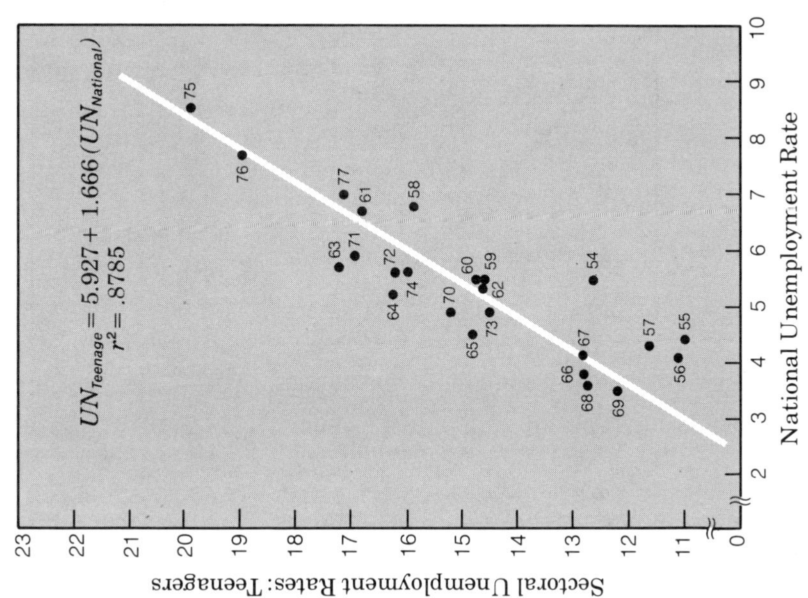
National Unemployment Rate
Sectoral Unemployment Rates: Teenagers
$UN_{Teenage} = 5.927 + 1.666\,(UN_{National})$
$r^2 = .8785$

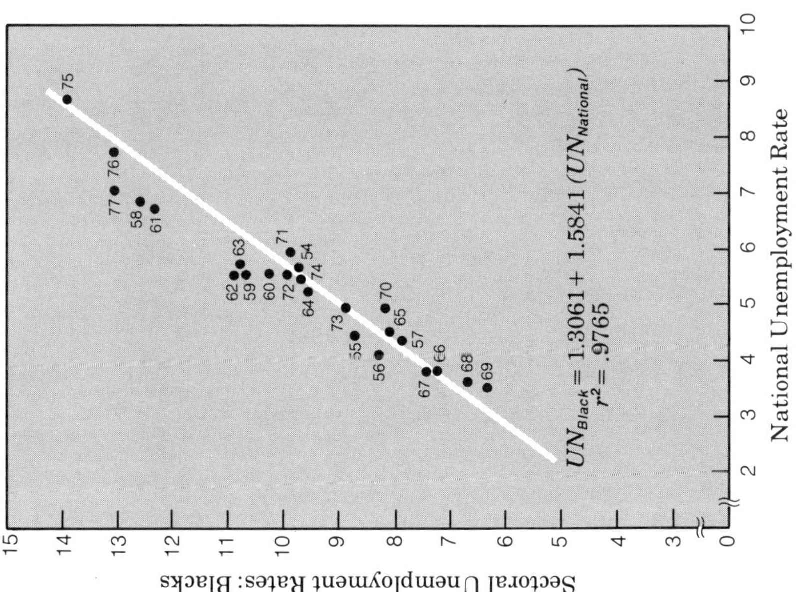
National Unemployment Rate
Sectoral Unemployment Rates: Blacks
$UN_{Black} = 1.3061 + 1.5841\,(UN_{National})$
$r^2 = .9765$

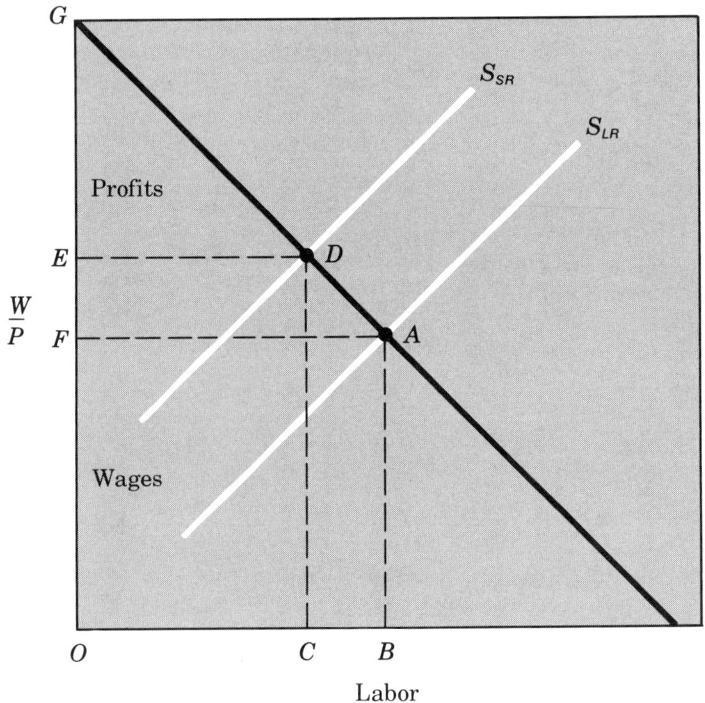
G
S_{SR}
S_{LR}
Profits
E
D
$\frac{W}{P}$
F
A
Wages
O
C
B
Labor

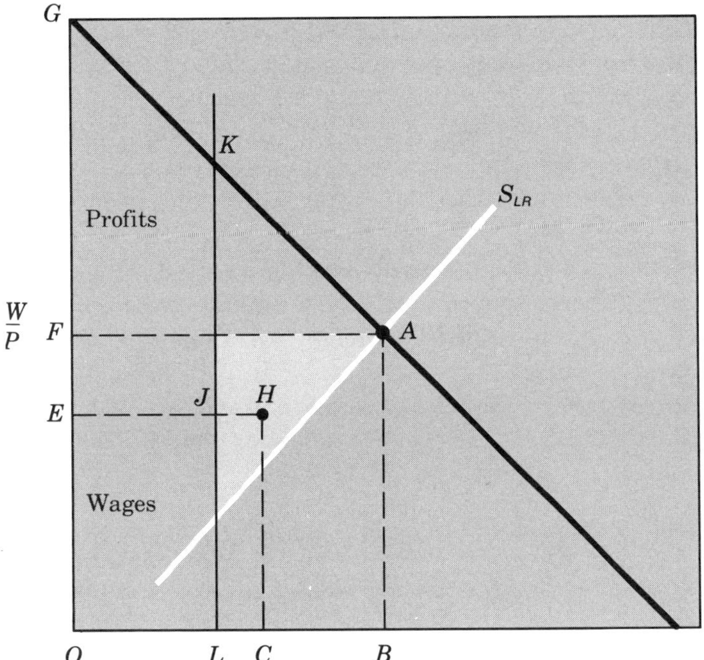

   Changes in the Distribution of Income

theories. One crude test is to compare the trend and actual real wage of all employed workers over the business cycle. According to the F-P theory, the real wage should rise in contractions and fall in booms, because of changes in labor productivity.

According to the ILM, the real wage should have a U-shaped relationship with output, peaking at the full employment level and falling in both recessions and booms. The data supports the ILM interpretation. In Figure 7.3a we have plotted annual rates of growth in the real wage in manufacturing against capacity utilization, and have fitted a regression line to the scatter of points. As the reader can see, the 1960s, a period of high capacity utilization, are years of high real wage gains, while the 1950s and the period starting in 1970 are contractionary periods of slow wage growth. The regression supports the ILM interpretation, for an increase of one percentage point in capacity utilization has been associated with a .26 percent rise in real wages in the United States. We can legitimately conclude that real wages are positively, not negatively, related to the level of economic activity, at least up to the kink in the aggregate supply curve.

Look next at the profit share, which we have plotted against capacity utilization in Figure 7.3b. The data leaves no doubt at all about the strong positive relationship between the profit share and the level of economic activity. According to the regression, a rise of one percentage point in capacity use has meant an increase of .15 percent in profits as a share of sales. Visually, it is clear that in every case, recession means a sharp drop in the share of profits, despite the fact that real wages of the labor force rise at less than average rates at the same time. The reason for that apparently paradoxical result is that labor productivity is strongly procyclical.[1] It goes up in booms and down in recessions, which is consistent with the labor stockpiling theory advanced by the ILM economists. Procyclical productivity movements have meant that, in booms, the real wage has gone up rapidly, and yet the real cost of labor has fallen—leading to a rise in profits.

---

[1] A regression of output/man hours, detrended, on capacity utilization shows the positive relationship. It yielded Q/H = .62 + .0045 CAP U, which says that output per man hour rises by .45% per one percent rise in capacity utilization.

     Inflation and Unemployment

Figure 7.3

Real Wages Profits and Capacity Utilization

Growth Rate of
Wages in Private
Non-farm Business

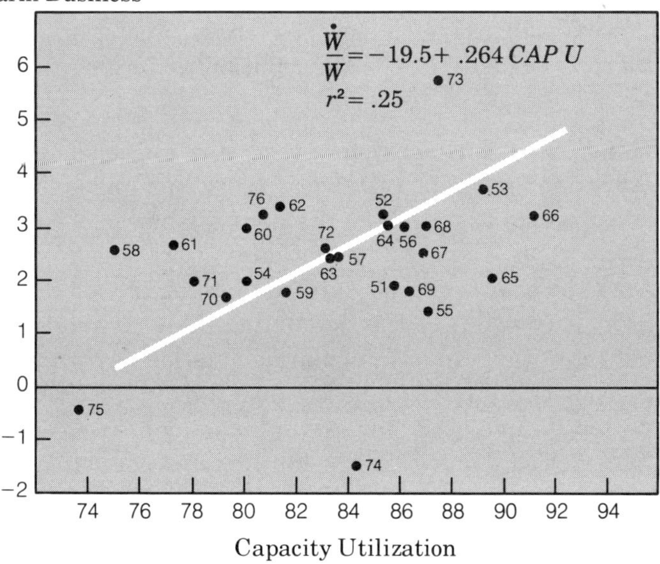

Profit Rate
(Before Taxes, as
a % of Sales)

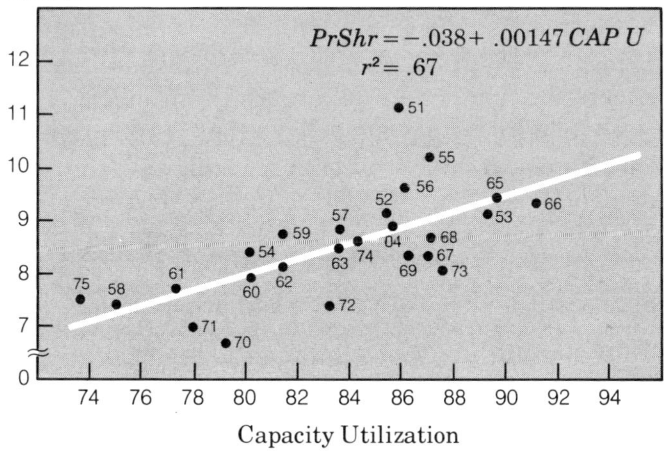

   Changes in the Distribution of Income

To summarize, the factor share and productivity data support the ILM model. All groups make absolute gains during booms and lose during recessions, but the relative gains and losses are not equally distributed. Because of stockpiling of skilled labor, it appears that the mainline labor force loses less than either profits or the marginal labor force during contractions. Hence we might expect the income share of skilled labor to rise in contractions and fall in booms, while the opposite should be true for both profits and marginal labor. Let us see how these predictions square with observed changes in the distribution of income in the United States.

While it was fairly easy to discern the influence of the level of economic activity on real wages, profits and unemployment rates, the influence of the cycle on the size distribution of income is much less clear-cut. The size distribution of income reported in Table 7.1 shows the shares of total personal income earned by various different percentiles of the population. Unfortunately, we cannot guarantee that any particular population class exactly corresponds to one of the four classes discussed in the previous section. The top income class, for example, undoubtedly contains many high salaried employees in addition to owners of capital. Nor is there a clear dividing line between either the mainline and marginal labor forces, or the marginal labor force and the nonworking poor. With these caveats in mind, let us look at the data.

At the bottom of the distribution a curious phenomenon has taken place in recent years. The bottom 20 percent has had a small but perceptible gain in its share since the mid-sixties. This is not due to employment gains in this group, but to steadily increasing welfare payments. This group is composed mainly of self-employed small farmers and families on welfare. Only 50 percent of their income comes from salary payments. In recent years a significant diversion of income from the rest of the population in the form of welfare payments has taken place. Since 1968 the fraction of GNP devoted to welfare has risen by a full percentage point, which is more than enough to explain the half percentage point increase in the income share of the bottom fifth of the U.S. population.

The second fifth of the population is the closest approximation provided by the distribution statistics to the marginal labor force. The income share of this group behaves exactly as predicted, rising

Table 7.1
Size Distribution of Income in the United States

Year	Bottom 20%	20-40%	40-80%	Top 20%	Top 5%	Capacity Utilization
1951	3.5	11.2	41.7	43.6	17.5	85.8
2	3.5	10.9	41.4	44.3	18.4	85.4
3	3.2	10.8	42.1	43.8	17.3	89.2
4	3.1	10.4	42.2	44.4	17.5	80.1
5	3.3	10.6	42.2	43.9	17.5	87.0
6	3.4	10.8	42.2	43.5	17.2	86.1
7	3.4	10.9	42.7	42.9	16.5	83.6
8	3.5	10.8	42.7	43.4	16.7	75.0
9	3.2	10.8	42.4	43.9	17.1	81.6
1960	3.2	10.6	42.3	44.0	17.0	80.1
1	3.1	10.6	41.8	44.9	17.7	77.3
2	3.4	10.2	42.3	43.9	16.8	81.4
3	3.4	10.4	42.3	43.9	16.9	83.5
4	3.4	10.4	42.1	44.1	17.2	85.7
5	3.6	10.6	42.3	43.6	16.6	89.5
6	3.8	10.7	42.2	43.4	16.7	91.1
7	3.6	10.6	42.3	43.4	16.5	86.9
8	3.8	10.7	42.1	43.5	16.8	87.0
9	3.7	10.5	42.1	43.7	16.8	86.2
1970	3.6	10.3	41.9	44.1	16.9	79.2
1	3.7	10.2	41.8	44.3	17.0	78.0
2	3.7	10.0	41.6	44.8	17.4	83.0
3	3.8	10.0	41.7	44.5	17.0	87.5
4	3.9	10.1	41.5	44.4	16.8	84.2
5	3.9	9.9	41.6	44.5	17.0	73.6

Source: U.S. Bureau of Census, *Consumer Income* (Washington, D.C., 1977).

in booms and falling in recessions. Its highest shares came during the Korean War and the mid-sixties boom, the lowest during the slack period of the early sixties and the seventies. This is the group whose relative position in the income pyramid has been most strongly affected by the level of economic activity in the United States.

Turning to the proxies for the mainline labor force and profits, we might arbitrarily assign the middle two fifths of the distribution (40-80 percent) as the former, and the top 20 percent as profits. As the reader can see, there is remarkable stability in the relative shares of these two groups over the postwar period. For the mainline labor force proxy, there is a slight tendency for the share to rise during the boom years of the sixties and to decline thereafter, while the opposite is true for the top 20 percent. Indeed the years since 1970, ones of fairly continual slack in the economy, have brought a steady redistribution away from the middle toward both the top and the bottom, despite the fact that profits have fallen during the recession. This has been caused by a significant increase in welfare payments during the 70s, benefiting the very bottom class and resulting in a rise in tax payments for the middle class. It also reflects an ability of wage earners at the top to maintain their real wages despite the slack in the economy. The mechanics of these high salary labor markets are not well understood and deserve further study, especially since they seem to be a significant explanatory factor in the concentration of income which has occurred during recent years.

There is one group which appears to gain uniformly from all stages of inflation—government. In Chapter 4 we showed how inflation increases tax receipts in real terms because of the progressivity of the tax system. In addition, inflation is a tax on holders of money. The government, as issuer of currency, collects that tax. The magnitude of the inflation tax can be very large indeed. In 1974, for example, the inflation rate was 11 percent. Full employment tax receipts of the federal government rose by $54 billion. Subtracting the effect of real output growth, the inflation caused a rise of $43 billion in tax receipts. Add to this the tax on currency holders. During 1974 outstanding currency was approximately $75 billion. Hence the tax on money was $8.25 billion (.11 x 75 = 8.25). Altogether, the inflation netted the government $43 + $8 = $51 billion in tax revenues. That represents an increase of 20 percent in taxes over 1973 full employment levels.

Inflation and the Uses of Income

We have concentrated so far on the effect of the level of economic activity on the distribution of earnings. Inflation has an indirect effect on this process through its effect on output and employment. But it is also possible that inflation could affect differently the real spending power of different groups. That is, the prices of the things the poor buy could rise by less or more than the prices of those bought by the rich. In that case, inflation would change the distribution of real purchasing power even if it did not affect the distribution of nominal income. Several recent studies have looked at this question by constructing a poor man's cost-of-living index. As one might expect, this index places a heavy weight on food and housing prices. Up through 1969 the poor man's price index rises by slightly less than the average consumer price index. This is especially true if the aged poor, with their high expenditures on medical care, are removed from the poor population. During the more recent period the situation has reversed. Rising food prices starting in 1973 and rising rents have pushed the poor man's price index to higher than average inflation rates. Overall, however, the differences are fairly small, and one may conclude that there is no systematic tendency for inflation to discriminate against the poor on the spending side.

Inflation and Wealth

Aside from its effect on income, inflation has important effects on the real value of wealth and its distribution. The prices of real assets such as land or houses tend to rise during inflations, thus protecting their owners against a potential loss of purchasing power. Fixed value assets such as currency, bonds, bank deposits or life insurance policies all fall in real terms.

In order to quantify the effect of inflation on the distribution of real wealth, it is first necessary to construct an inventory of assets by income class, and then estimate the likely price reaction of each asset to inflation. One recent study has attempted to do this and we summarize its results.[2]

The poor are by and large debtors. Debtors gain during the expansionary phase of an inflation because interest rates will not fully reflect rising prices. Hence the real cost of repaying loans will fall. However, as lenders learn about inflation and raise their rates, this redistribution from creditor to debtor should largely disappear.

As we proceed up the income distribution, the asset-debt ratio rises. This rise would lead us to expect that the initial or expansionary phase of an inflation would tend to equalize the distribu-

---

[2] E. C. Budd and D. F. Seiders, "The Impact of Inflation on the Distribution of Income and Wealth," *American Economic Review*, 61 (May 1971), 128–139.

tion of real wealth; that is, unexpected inflation should act like a tax on the wealthy, which is exactly what Budd and Seiders found in their recent study.

One might ask: what about common stocks? It used to be an adage on Wall Street that when an inflation was expected an investor purchased common stocks. Stocks, after all, represent title to machines and other real assets whose earning power should increase along with prices. Since the ownership of common stock is concentrated in the upper income groups, this could offset the equalizing effect of inflation on real wealth. Note two points in this regard. First, and most importantly, there is no necessary relationship between stock prices and inflation, as investors have found to their sorrow in the years since 1970. Second, Budd and Seiders, in the study to which we just referred, did assume that stock prices rose in real terms. Even at that, the wealthy lost in relation to the poor.

But is it obvious that stock prices must rise in inflations? As so often before, we must distinguish between the expansionary and the stabilization phases. During expansion, profits rise and wealth holders switch from fixed-value assets such as bonds to stocks. Stock prices rise. During stabilization it is a different matter. Corporate earnings fall as we have seen, and the decrease reduces stock prices. In addition, it is evident that government policy-makers fear inflation. In their attempt to control it, they typically use restrictive monetary policy. The Federal Reserve sells bonds and this drives bond prices down and interest rates up. Bonds and stocks are substitute ways of holding wealth. When bond rates rise, the increase makes bonds attractive in relation to stocks. Prices of stocks fall as the public switches into higher yielding bonds. In recent years, therefore, news of inflation has had a depressing effect on Wall Street. That is because investors correctly, it has turned out, expect inflation to be followed by contractionary monetary policy. It is not the inflation itself, but the prescribed cure for it, which has driven investors out of the stock market in recent years.

To summarize all of this discussion, it would appear that the effect of inflation on the distribution of wealth is complementary with its effect on the distribution of earnings. The expansionary phase is progressive, both because the poor find jobs and because unexpected inflation is beneficial to the poor as debtors. Stabilization reverses these gains unless mitigated by rising transfer payments as has been the case in the United States.

Conclusion

When we review the entire discussion of the effect of inflation and the level of economic activity on the distribution of income, the recurrent theme which stands out is that no group but the government gains uniformly throughout the inflationary process. Groups like the marginal labor force or business which gain the most during expansion lose the most during stabilization. Thus, over the inflationary cycle, there seem to be no permanent winners or losers, only survivors.

The reason for our conclusion is the connection between the different parts of the inflationary cycle or process. Because stabilizations follow expansions no group gains from inflation. If there were a way for the economy to have expansion without a gradual acceleration of inflation, groups such as the marginal labor force could benefit, because a government could choose a point on a short-run Phillips curve with a low level of unemployment. Inflation would be a way of reducing the inequality of the income distribution and of permanently helping the poor. Our theory, however, suggests that it is not possible to stay at points below the long-run unemployment rate without running the risk of ever-accelerating inflation. Consequently, in the United States, whenever such a point has been reached, the government has immediately stabilized with significant costs both to the working poor and even to the middle class.

Yet we do not really know how fast the adjustment of expectations occurs. One would have to agree with Hollister and Palmer[3] that we have spent most of the postwar period finding out about the relationship between inflation and high levels of unemployment at great cost to the poor, particularly the working poor. Yet we have very few observations in the low unemployment range. Thus we really do not know how fast the economy would drift up from the short-run Phillips curve. We do not know how long an inflationary

---

[3]   Hollister and Palmer, *op. cit.*

expansion could last before the acceleration of price inflation demanded a change in policy, because we have always stabilized at the first sign of inflation. How many years, for example, could the U.S. economy have maintained the 1967 unemployment rate of 3.8 percent before the inflation rate became unacceptable? We do not know. And this is unfortunate because, if the inflation generated by this level of unemployment were moderate, there need be little acceleration. Under these conditions, cautious expansion would be a viable way of permanently reducing poverty and providing jobs to the working poor in the United States.

Questions

1. Why don't creditors necessarily lose, and debtors necessarily gain, during an inflation?
2. Why would we expect the government's share of real GNP to increase during both stages of an inflation? Under what conditions would the government's share not increase? Could it ever decrease?
3. We have indicated in this chapter that many groups which are harmed (helped) during the expansion stage of an inflation are helped (harmed) during the stabilization phase. If the real income losses are eventually more or less balanced by real income gains, why should policymakers be concerned about inflation?
4. Why can't our theory predict what happens to factor shares during an inflation? What additional information would be necessary in order to make such predictions?
5. Why, if stocks are such good inflation hedges, has the stock market in recent years generally fallen on news that inflation rates are rising?
6. What is the difference between the Neoclassical and the ILM predictions on the distributional impact of recession?

Suggestions for Further Reading

Bach, George L., and Albert Ando, "The Redistributional Effects of Inflation," *Review of Economics and Statistics* (February 1957), 1–13.

Bach, George L., and James B. Stephenson, "Inflation and the Redistribution of Wealth," *Review of Economics and Statistics* (February 1974), 1–13.

Budd, Edward C., and David F. Seiders, "The Impact of Inflation on the Distribution of Income and Wealth," *American Economic Review* (May 1971), 128–139.

Hollister, Robinson, and John L. Palmer, "The Impact of Inflation on the Poor," University of Wisconsin, Institute for Research on Poverty #40, 1969.

Kessel, Reuben A., "Inflation Caused Wealth Redistribution: A Hypothesis," *American Economic Review* (March 1956), 128–141.

Metcalf, Charles E., "The Size Distribution of Personal Income During the Business Cycle," *American Economic Review* (September 1969), 657–667.

Nordhaus, William D., "The Effects of Inflation on the Distribution of Economic Welfare," *Journal of Money, Credit and Banking* (February 1973), 465–504.

Chapter Eight

The Problem of Stabilization

Stabilizing an economy after a period of inflation is probably the most delicate and difficult economic maneuver that a government can attempt. Stabilization at such a time means inevitably a cutting back in some direction—someone's spending and consumption must fall; someone must lose his job. It is the morning after an economic blast. Are there better and worse ways to get through this unpleasant morning-after?

The goal of stabilization is to return to a desired rate of increase in prices, with the least possible loss in production during the transition period. The government has several key decisions to make. Most important is whether to stabilize using orthodox policies of demand reduction or price and wage controls. We will discuss the merits of each in this chapter. But prior to deciding how to get there, the government must decide where it is trying to go—it must choose a target rate of inflation. In making that choice, the cost of stabilization must be balanced against the cost of inflation. The cost of stabilization through demand reduction is a period of dislocation, falling output, and high unemployment. Stabilizing by price and wage controls is costly in terms of government bureaucracy and of the possibility of inefficient and inequitable price and wage decisions. In the United States during recent years we have found this cost to be high.

What are the costs of inflation? Why not simply accept whatever rate is being forecast by labor and adjust the entire system to it? Not attempting to reduce expected inflation is a policy alternative which deserves to be seriously considered, especially if the costs of inflation are judged to be small.

One cost of inflation is that it causes the economic system to operate inefficiently. In Chapter 2 we showed how inflation induces people to reduce their money holdings and to change their saving behavior in ways that make less productive capital available to the economy. People devote time, and business devotes labor, to avert inflationary redistributions of real wealth. Such action is inefficient. Moreover, inflation is discriminatory. Unless inflation is perfectly anticipated, it can cause rather dramatic changes in real income shares in the short run. These attributes are undesirable.

The government has to balance the inefficiencies and inequities introduced by an inflation against the temporary costs of reducing the inflation to some desired level. Quite clearly, the longer the inflation continues, the longer will be the period of adjustment to a lower actual rate. The reason for this is that the public, and especially labor, have become accustomed to that historic rate of inflation. They will expect it to continue in the future, and it will take some time before their expectations adjust to the lower rate. During the adjustment period the levels of output and employment are undoubtedly going to be less than normal, because actual real wages rise above their long-run equilibrium levels.

Once again we should stress the fundamental difference between stabilization with zero and positive expected inflation. When labor expects no future change in prices, wages need rise only enough to offset previous inflation. There is a one-time further increase in prices, an elimination of involuntary overemployment, and the process ends. There is no period of more than normal unemployment, no period of excess capacity. Stabilization involves nothing more than giving up greater-than-normal output levels.

When inflationary expectations have become embedded in wage decisions, the cost of stabilization rises dramatically. Now the government, in its attempt to stabilize, must produce an actual rate of inflation lower than expected. We have not learned any other way of doing this except through a temporary recession. Thus, if an inflation has gone on long enough so that expected inflation is positive, the public must expect stabilization to lead to a period of greater than normal unemployment, excess capacity and unused resources, while the economy adjusts to the lower rate. The longer the inflation, the higher the likely unemployment during stabilization.

Our analysis implies that the cost and the difficulty of stabilizing vary directly with the length of the preceding inflation and the degree of price rigidity in the economy. There must be cases where the history of inflation is so long or price inflexibility so high that stabilization per se is not an optimal policy. That is, the cost of continuing the inflation may well be less than the cost of stabilizing. It may then be wiser to adapt the economy to the inflation by introducing automatic escalators in all wage and mortgage contracts rather than attempt to eliminate the inflation through an extended period of unemployment. Price stability is not an end in itself. It is just one characteristic of an economy whose benefits may or may not be worth the cost of achievement.

Suppose that the government has decided on a target rate of inflation lower than the one expected by the labor force. The problem is to drive wages, prices and expectations down to that target level. There are two fundamentally different ways of doing this: 1) reducing aggregate demand through restrictive monetary and fiscal policy and 2) wage and/or price controls. Which policy is preferable depends upon the shape of the short-run aggregate supply curve. Those who favor restrictive monetary and fiscal policy believe that the supply curve is upward sloping, those who favor controls believe that it is flat. Let us now consider these two alternative programs in more detail and the conditions under which one or the other is to be preferred.

Stabilization by Reducing Aggregate Demand

The orthodox way of reducing the rate of inflation is

by lowering the level of aggregate demand through some combination of higher taxes, lower government spending or a reduction in the money supply. This will shift the aggregate demand curve of the economy to the left (Figure 8.1). Business will find that it cannot sell its output for as high a price as it could have if the government had not reduced demand. Rates of inflation decline. At the new price level, business will find it unprofitable to hire laborers whose wage demands are now unrealistically high, given the new lowered rate of inflation. After a period in which rates of inflation are lower than those expected by labor, the unemployed workers begin to lower their expectations and their wage demands. This puts pressure on the wage rates of the workers who are still employed, and the average rate of increase of wages begins to decline. In terms of the Phillips curve, reducing aggregate demand moves the economy to the right along a short-run Phillips curve (from A to B in Figure 8.2). As expectations adjust downward, wage demands decline, employment begins to rise, and the stabilization phase draws to a close. (The economy moves clockwise down the dotted path from B to C in Figure 8.2.)

The Effect of Orthodox Stabilization in an ILM Economy

We have seen in previous chapters that there is a significant disagreement among economists about the shape of the short-run supply and Phillips curves. Because of markup pricing, monopoly power, and labor stockpiling, there may be a kink in both of these curves, such that both become flat at less than full employment (see Figure 8.3).

When demand is reduced below D_1, the economy moves out along the flat part of the supply and Phillips curves to B. The inflation rate does not fall but unemployment increases dramatically. One would expect that the presence of supernormal unemployment at B would lead employed workers to moderate wage demands, allowing prices to decline. But that, as we have seen, is not the way things seem to work. When there is a recession, companies do not lay off their skilled labor in proportion to the decline in output that they suffer. If they expect the downturn to be a short one, it is cheaper for them to maintain their skilled labor force even though some of the workers are partially idle in the short run. This can be

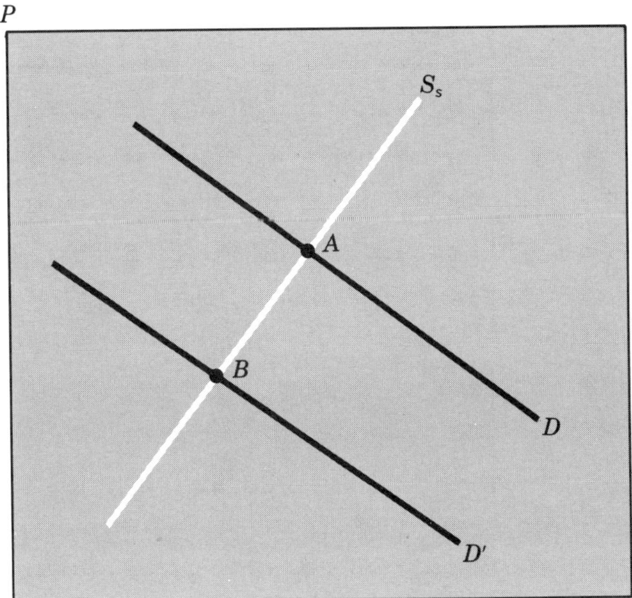
P
S_s
A
B
D
D'
Real Income

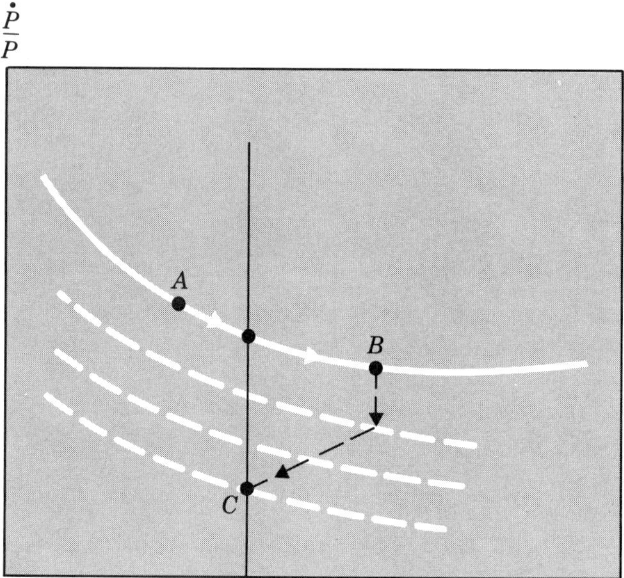

    Inflation and Unemployment

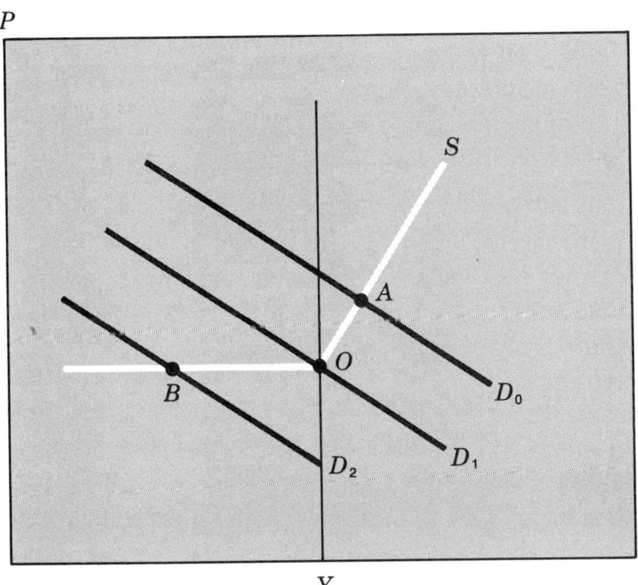

Phillips Curve

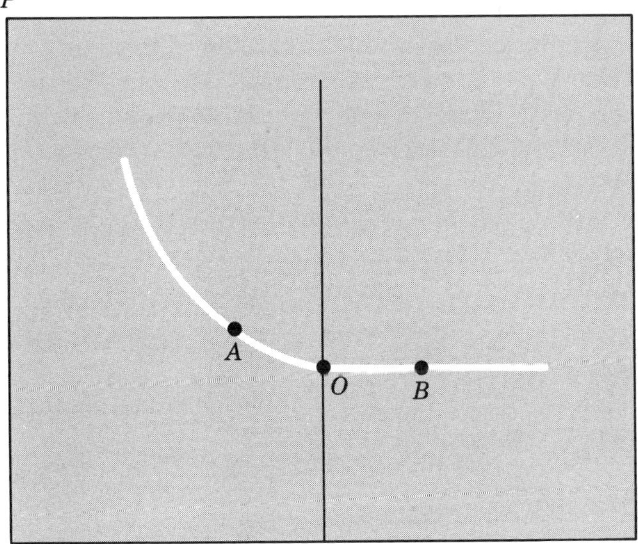

explained by the importance of firm-specific training in the skilled labor force. During recessions, therefore, the unemployment rate of skilled labor remains quite low. Big increases in unemployment occur among the marginal labor force, but that does not put much pressure on the wages of skilled workers. With excess labor already, companies simply stop hiring. That is, they engage in job rationing at the going wage, rather than driving wages down and hiring the unemployed.

If the short-run aggregate supply curve is kinked for these or some other reasons, orthodox stabilization to drive down inflation rates does not make sense unless the economy is operating above the kink. In Figure 8.3, reducing demand from D_0 to D_1 will lower the inflation rate, but going on to D_2 only drives up the unemployment rate and causes a recession. It has no effect on either inflation or expectations. For if prices and wages are not flexible downward, the entire effect of the stabilization program will be reflected in reductions in output and employment, not prices. Inflexible prices turn an intended deflation of prices into a depression of output. Clearly, the flatter the supply curve of the economy, the more severe will be the real costs of orthodox stabilization in terms of lost output, unemployed people and wasted resources. The dimensions of this cost are enormous.

Since 1968 the United States has been almost continuously engaged in an attempt to slow down what I have labeled the Vietnam War inflation. From 1970, when the stabilization first took hold, onward to the end of 1976, the United States has been in a recession for 19 of the 28 quarters in the period.[1] During that same period, the difference between the actual output of the economy, and what it could have produced at full employment, amounts to over $400 billion. We have already paid a very big price for inflation control. If prices are inflexible, most of that lost output really has been wasted in a fruitless application of the wrong policy.

It should be obvious that the extent of wage and price rigidity in an economy is an extremely important empirical question which should be decided upon before a stabilization strategy is chosen.

---

[1] We are defining *recession* here as operating at less than 83 percent of manufacturing capacity.

And yet, considering its importance, surprisingly little empirical work has been done on wage and/or price rigidity. As we saw in Chapter 4, most of the evidence suggests relatively rigid or inflexible prices. Most of the people who support orthodox stabilization assume that there is a positive relationship between demand and prices. They would be surprised to learn how weak and uncertain that relationship appears to be.

Another factor which is relevant to the debate on the relative flexibility of prices and wages is the degree of unemployment. Probably few of the proponents of wage and price rigidity would care to argue that prices and wages would remain inflexible in the face of really severe unemployment. That is, if national unemployment rates were driven to 20 percent as they were in the 1930s, we undoubtedly would see wage and price reductions. But no policymaker is willing to put the economy through such an economic wringer. The political and economic price would be too high. Therefore we have mild recessions instead. National unemployment rates have not been allowed to exceed 9 percent. While that rate implies severe unemployment for subgroups of the population, it apparently does not produce a high enough unemployment rate among skilled workers to significantly affect wage negotiations. The political implications of unemployment are severe enough to demand a stop to stabilization before the point where that unemployment has a large economic impact. Thus, believers in inflexible wages and prices are really arguing for inflexibility over the range relevant to policymakers. The Phillips curve is flat out to the furthest unemployment rate that our policymakers are willing to explore.

If wages and prices are sticky downward within the politically feasible ranges of unemployment, orthodox stabilization is not a sensible policy beyond a certain point, for it won't reduce prices and will cause a recession. The best known alternative inflation program is a system of wage and price controls. We now consider some of the general programs which have been proposed.

Wage and Price Controls

What we mean by a wage-price control program is some intervention by the government to force labor and management to set prices and wages below the level they would otherwise have chosen. The aim of the intervention is to bring the rate of inflation down to an acceptable level without the necessity of an unemployment-producing recession. In terms of our supply and Phillips curve diagrams, the government forces the economy down from one flat supply or Phillips curve to a lower one. Under the orthodox stabilization, this downward motion is supposed to come about through the pressure of the unemployed and idle capacity upon wages and prices.

No one particularly likes wage and price controls. They mean government bureaucracy, inefficiencies, shortages, prices set at the wrong level, etc. Advocates simply believe that these costs are less than those of any alternative anti-inflation program. Consider now the general kinds of programs that have been proposed. Disregarding voluntary guidelines, there are two types of program, one of which controls prices and wages, and the other which controls only wages. Since wage controls are common to both, let us first consider the wage component of a control system.

The general form of most of the wage control systems that have been proposed is that average wages for each firm should be allowed to rise at the national rate of increase of productivity plus the target rate of inflation. If such a policy were strictly adhered to, and if there were no increase in profit margins, the actual inflation rate would equal the target rate.[2] Thus, if the price controllers want to arrive at a 2.5 percent rate of inflation, and if they expect labor productivity to rise by 3 percent per year, they allow wages to rise by 5.5 percent. Labor costs, prices and profits all rise by 2.5 percent. Note that under this formula profits remain constant in real terms.

But we know that there are intra-sectoral differences in productivity. Should not the wage increase granted to workers in each sector reflect this? The answer appears to be no, but over the long run there should not be too much difference between the two systems. Under either system we should note that wages must

$$^2 P = \pi + WL$$

$$L = \frac{1}{APL}$$

$$\pi = \lambda P$$

$$\text{hence } \frac{\dot{P}}{P} = \frac{\lambda \dot{P}}{P} + (1-\lambda)\frac{\dot{WL}}{WL}$$

$$\text{or } \frac{\dot{P}}{P} = \frac{\dot{W}}{W} - \frac{\dot{APL}}{APL}$$

P = Price
π = Profits
W = Wage
L = Labor inputs
APL = Averge product of labor
λ = Profit share

reflect supply and demand conditions in the labor market as well as productivity. Under the uniform productivity rule, wage costs and relative prices rise in low productivity sectors. That means that either prices fall or profits rise in high productivity sectors. In either case capital, production, and jobs gradually flow from the low to the high productivity areas of the economy. Relative profits and prices encourage both consumers and producers to take advantage of variations in productivity across sectors.

When wages follow sectoral rather than national productivity trends, the adjustment is shifted from prices and profits to wages. If wages rise with productivity in each sector, neither relative prices nor profits change. Rather wages rise in high productivity sectors. This should draw workers away from low productivity areas—tending to equalize wages and expand output in the more productive sectors of the economy.

Thus it would appear that the final effect of the two different wage systems on the economy is the same—output and employment shifting toward the more productive sectors. However, the paths followed and the beneficiaries are different. Under the national rule, consumers and capitalists benefit from differential productivity, workers do not. Under the sectoral productivity rule, the opposite is true. In the first case, the force for expansion is consumer demand and relative profit rates; in the latter, the attraction of high relative wages on sectoral labor supply. Whether one prefers the national or the sectoral system depends upon whether one wants workers or consumers to benefit from changes in productivity in the short run.

We now turn to a far more complex question—price controls. Before one even starts thinking about the design of any program, it is good to recognize a few fundamental facts about prices and the price system. Prices are the basic transmitter of information in a market economy. They are signals, telling producers about the desires of consumers. As such, they play a central role in the allocation of the economy's productive resources. Any price control system will make prices lower than they would have been in the open market. Employment and output decisions will be affected. There should be compelling reasons for intervention in such a key element of our economic system.

Deciding upon the right price or the right system of prices is an incredibly difficult job. The government must keep track of literally millions of price and wage decisions. It has to know the "right" level for each price, and how that level should change over time. Suppose, for example, that the government sets a target rate of inflation of 4 percent. Does this mean that all prices should be rising by 4 percent? Not at all. If there is any real growth going on in the economy, some products are expanding. Even in the absence of any greater than normal price increases in the raw material costs or wages, prices may rise in the industry because of diminishing returns. How much they rise depends on just how hard it is to expand output. In a growing economy the demand for different products grows at different rates, and the ability to supply that increased demand varies by industry. The government would have to know each industry's supply curve to determine the justifiable price increase it should be granted. Another problem immediately comes to mind. What signal does the market have for raising output other than profits? If demand rises in an industry, prices are raised, profits increase, and business in that industry is prompted to expand its facilities and to increase its output. The short-run rise in prices is the legitimate signaling device of the market economy by which more output will later be supplied. If the government short-circuits the signal, no extra output will be forthcoming. This is all right if government sets the right price. If it sets one that is too low, the substitute for inflation is a smaller total output and perhaps rationing. One sees examples of this in public utilities and cities with rent controls. Prices set at artificially low levels have created long-run shortages in electric power, natural gas, and housing.

Yet other problems with price controls are the possibilities of cheating and customer discrimination that are introduced. Manufacturers can downgrade the quality of their products to cut costs when prices are set at the wrong level. They can create new products for which no price controls exist and stop making the old products. An amusing example of this occurred in the United States in 1972. Price controls were applied to 4x8 plywood sheets. In response, the plywood manufacturers cut 1/16 inch off their sheets and started selling a new product, 4x7-15/16 plywood sheets, for which there was no price ceiling. They also exported lumber to

Canada, where the prices were higher, and then bought it back again because price controls did not apply on imported products. There is probably no system that could be devised which would eliminate all such loopholes.

Because of the enormous complexity of the economy, all feasible price control programs limit their coverage in one way or another. Typically the limitations are either by the importance of the product or by the degree of monopoly power of the firm producing the product. Since there is a crude relationship between monopoly power, or price setting ability, and firm size, most programs reserve the closest scrutiny for the largest firms. The argument is that, since prices are administered in such firms anyway, one might as well substitute a public for a private administrator. He or she at least has the public interest in mind when price decisions are made.

Suppose that the government has selected the group of firms whose prices are to be monitored. What criteria should it use in setting the firm's prices? For example, do we let the firm pass on all costs on a dollar-for-dollar basis or on a percentage basis? The former will keep dollar profits constant, while the latter will allow profits to grow at the same percentage rate as costs. The disadvantage of the latter is that it gives the firm an incentive to be inefficient. All it must do is show a cost increase, whether this be executive airplanes, paneling in corporate headquarters or a wasteful use of labor, in order to get permission to raise prices and profits. Cost pass-through on a dollar-for-dollar basis is a system by which prices are allowed to rise only by the same number of dollars that cost per dollar of sales goes up. Thus, if labor and raw material costs amount to 75 percent of sales, and if they rise by 10 percent, product prices will be allowed to rise only by 7.5 percent. Profits per dollar of sales are thus constant. The only problem with this rule is that it penalizes profits if there is general inflation. Profits after all represent the payment for capital and entrepreneurial services. They must be sufficient to cover depreciation and to induce businesspeople to take risks. Some adjustment of nominal profits must therefore be allowed under general inflation even if full cost pass-through is not permitted.

Because of the administrative difficulties encountered in operating a full-fledged price and wage control system, several economists have recently proposed some interesting alternatives. They suggest using tax incentives or penalties to encourage wage restraint by business.[2] The essential idea is to set allowable wage increases according to a norm, such as desired or expected inflation plus productivity, and then to impose penalty taxes on corporations whose wages exceed this level.

The attraction of such a scheme is that it does not require an extensive bureaucracy. Each corporation simply counts up its employees, and multiplies that number times its permissible average wage level. That will be the average paid the previous year plus the permissible wage increase set by the federal government. Wages above that level trigger a penalty tax. Administratively there are certain problems, such as what to do about new firms, or firms whose employment structure changes, but these do not appear incapable of solution. The big advantage of such a scheme is that it proposes a way to stop inflation without extensive interference in the price system and yet without imposing undue sacrifice on anyone. The flexibility of freely fluctuating relative prices is retained, bureaucracy is minimized, and yet inflation can be controlled without a recession.

As we said at the outset of this chapter, stabilization is unpleasant. No one likes recessions, wage controls or the continuation of inflation. One chooses a stabilization policy so as to limit the damage caused by moving to lower inflation rates. We have offered some general principles which should govern this choice. Controls are preferable to demand management if prices and/or wages are inflexible downward. A plan based on tax penalties for excessive wage settlements is another promising alternative way to solve the inflation problem at a relatively low cost.

Since we do not know precisely what sort of an economic environment we are in, there is widespread disagreement over the appropriate stabilization policies. During the last eight years the United States has tried practically every policy outlined in this

----

[2] A plan based on penalties is the Wallich-Weintraub plan; see Sidney Weintraub, *Capitalism's Inflation and Unemployment Crisis* (Reading, Mass.: Addison-Wesley, 1978), ch. 6.

Arthur Okun has proposed a plan based on tax incentives; see Arthur Okun, "The Great Stagflation Swamp," *Challenge* (November–December 1977), p. 13.

chapter. None of the policies can be called an unqualified success.
The rate of inflation has stubbornly resisted our best efforts to
bring it to lower levels. How to stabilize an economy is, unfortunately, still an open question in economics.

Questions

1. What is the relationship between the shape of the
   aggregate supply curve and stabilization policy?
2. Describe the theory on which orthodox stabilization is
   based. Why is a recession usually required to reduce the
   inflation rate according to this theory?
3. Throughout this book we have characterized inflation
   as a more or less short-run phenomenon. Yet some
   countries, such as Chile, have experienced continuous
   and high rates of inflation for decades. Can such an
   apparent paradox be explained within the framework of
   the theory presented?
4. Would cost-of-living escalator clauses be inflationary?
5. In 1962 President John F. Kennedy prevented the steel
   industry from raising its prices. Was this action
   anti-inflationary? Is there a difference between the
   short-run and the long-run effects of the policy?
6. Suppose you were going to institute a system of price
   controls. Would you allow any price increases? Would
   you make exceptions for firms that are increasing their
   output? How would you decide the "right" price for each
   industry?

Suggestions for Further Reading

Galbraith, John K., "Market Structure and Stabilization
Policy," *Review of Economics and Statistics* (May 1957),
124–133.

Modigliani, Franco, "The Monetarist Controversy or,
Should We Forsake Stabilization Policies," *American
Economic Review* (March 1977), 1–19

Okun, Arthur M., "The Great Stagflation Swamp,"
Challenge (November-December 1977), 6–14.

Schultz, George., and Robert Z. Aliber, *Guidelines,
Informal Controls and the Market Place*. Chicago:
University of Chicago Press, 1966.

Smithies, Arthur, "The Control of Inflation," *Review of
Economics and Statistics* (August 1957), 272–283.

Ulman, Lloyd, and Robert J. Flanagan, *Wage Restraint: A Study of Incomes Policies in Western Europe*. Berkeley: University of California Press, 1971.

Chapter Nine

Stabilization in the United States, 1967-76

The period since 1967 offers an invaluable lesson in the practice of stabilization. During this nine-year period most of the policies we have discussed in the last chapter have been tried in a long and frustrating battle with increasing prices. The record shows with depressing clarity how hard it is to stabilize an economy, once a serious inflation has been allowed to continue long enough to affect peoples' expectations. Despite five years of recession, and $450 billion of lost output, the inflation rate is higher in 1977 than it was ten years earlier when the stabilization began. In this chapter we will briefly describe the U.S. stabilization effort and draw some tentative conclusions and lessons from it.

The 1960s were a time of great hopes followed by bitter disappointment for economic policymakers. In 1966 their reputations had never been higher. By a judicious use of tax cuts, budget deficits and expansionary monetary policy, they had apparently broken the inevitable boom-recession business cycle. In December 1965 the economy was entering its 58th month of economic expansion, the longest peacetime boom in U.S. history. Unemployment was down to 4.1

percent, the lowest rate since 1957, and profits were at their highest levels since the Korean War. Yet the rate of inflation was less than 2 percent. One could have been forgiven for believing that the United States was entering a new era of progress and uninterrrupted prosperity.

Unfortunately, it was not to be. The Vietnam War and our government's unwillingness to ask U.S. citizens to pay for it changed everything. We strayed off the delicate line between full employment and excess demand and are still trying to recover from that misstep.

The war came at a most unpropitious time. The economy by 1965 was already at or close to full employment. This was not a time when a major new government spending program could be introduced without either a contraction in some other area or an increase in taxes. But President Johnson was unwilling to cut his Great Society programs because of the war. Thus, while defense expenditures were rising by 57 percent in the period 1965–68, Federal transfer payments were rising by a not much smaller 51 percent. We now know that as early as 1965, government economists began pushing for an increase in taxes. The government delayed, apparently because it believed its own propaganda that the war would be a short one, and because it wished to hide the cost of an unpopular war from the American people. The result was a rise of Federal government expenditures in real terms by over 25 percent, 1965– 67, and a corresponding increase of $14 billion in the Federal deficit. These fiscal developments helped to fuel a large increase in aggregate demand at a time when the economy had little idle capacity in either workers or machines. In such a scenario there can be only one outcome. The rate of inflation rose ominously in 1966 and again in 1967, capacity utilization rose to over 90 percent, and the unemployment rate fell below 4 percent for the first time since the Korean War.

Belatedly the government mobilized to fight the inflation. Its first actions were traditional orthodox demand restraint. Both fiscal and monetary policy were used. Because the fiscal authorities were reluctant to request a tax increase in 1966, for political reasons, the monetary authorities were the first to act. In the early months of 1966, they produced a short, but sharp, contraction in the nation's money supply. Six months later there was an unmistakable slowing down in demand and production. What would have happened had the Federal Reserve maintained its restrictive stance is a fascinating question that we will never answer satisfactorily because the Federal Reserve backed off. The money supply, which had grown only 2.2 percent in 1966, was allowed to grow by 6.6 percent in 1967 and 7.2 percent in 1968.

Meanwhile the government had reluctantly come to the conclusion that an increase in taxes was necessary. In his Economic Report for 1967, President Johnson asked Congress to enact a temporary 10 percent income surtax. Despite the mounting evidence of inflationary pressure in the economy, the bill was not signed until June 1968. Even though the tax was retroactive to January for corporations and April for individuals, a full year went by between the request for the surtax and its implementation by a reluctant Congress. And this was only one of a series of lags between the time when the tax was first needed and the time when it finally affected spending. For during the final quarters of 1968 and the first quarters of 1969, the public reacted to the new surtax by reducing saving, not consumption. There was a very good reason for this. The tax was announced as temporary. Households had the choice of reducing purchases during the period of the tax by the full amount of the tax or spreading that reduction over a number of years by reducing both consumption and saving. Because savings provide for consumption in future years, by reducing savings households could, in effect, spread the reduced consumption over a number of years, which is surely a rational thing to do. Eventually, as the surtax was extended for a full year to June 1970, private consumption did fall, a major factor in the downturn in economic activity that began in the fourth quarter of 1969. But the lag between the first presentation of the tax surcharge and its effect spread over two years. During that time the consumer price index rose by 11 percent. A policy which is that slow is not a very effective stabilization tool.

As we have seen, during the two years 1967 and 1968, the monetary authorities had permitted an expansionary monetary policy. In 1969, as inflation accelerated, they switched back to restraint. During the eight months from July 1969 through February 1970, the money supply rose by less than .5 percent, which meant a decline of 3 percent in real terms. Interest rates soared to their highest levels in over one hundred years. Finally, fiscal and monetary policy were pulling in the same direction, and both were working strongly toward restraint. Slowly demand began to contract. Throughout 1969 the rate of growth of the economy fell while unemployment held at the abnormally low level of 3.5–3.8 percent. Inflation worsened significantly. In 1970 the induced recession began in earnest. Unemployment rates climbed rapidly throughout the year, going from 3.5 percent in December 1969 to 6.2 percent one year later. Gross national product declined in real terms. Monetary and fiscal policy had successfully broken the boom by reducing aggregate demand.

Driving the country into a recession was not the final goal of government stabilizers. They saw the recession as an unpleasant first step toward the achievement of a lower rate of inflation. It was fairly clear that the delays in imposing restraint, coupled with massive Vietnam War expenditures, had generated the worst inflation of the postwar period. Here in the words of the Council of Economic Advisers is how they expected the policy to work.[1]

> The slowdown in the growth of purchases (because of restrictive monetary and fiscal policy) would mean a slowdown in the growth of sales; more sluggish market conditions would encourage businesses to pursue temperate pricing policies, especially as this influence began to be reinforced by a slowdown in the rise of wage rates and unit labor costs. The reductions in wage and price increases would tend to reinforce each other. The longer price increases moderated, the weaker would become the expectation of further inflation. In turn, business and labor would be increasingly inclined to respond to the waning inflation by making appropriate price and wage adjustments, in preference to accepting a lower volume of production and less employment. With this change the economy would be on the road to regaining full employment without setting off another round of inflation.

In other words, the Council saw unemployment and recession as a way of reducing the rate of actual inflation and thus bringing expected inflation to a lower rate. Once expectations had fallen to an acceptable level, the economy would be allowed to return to full employment.

[1] *Economic Report of the President* (Washington, D.C., 1971), p. 27.

For more than eighteen months the government resolutely played by this orthodox game plan. At first it was gratified by reductions in the rate of inflation. The seasonally adjusted annual rate of increase of the Consumer Price Index, which had been 5.9 percent in the second half of 1969 and 6.0 percent in the first half of 1970, was 4.6 percent from June to November (1970). More worrisome, unemployment rose to a reported 6 percent of the labor force by December. These kinds of unemployment rates cannot be maintained unless they yield fairly quick results in reductions in wage and price increases. And that did not seem to be happening. Listen to the Council of Economic Advisers again.[2]

> The behavior of prices from the end of 1970 to mid August (1971) and especially after April heightened concern about inflation. Although the rise in consumer prices continued to decelerate for several months early in the year, it quickened in the spring, as did the rise in wholesale industrial prices. . . . The 1970 improvement (in the CPI) had been due mainly to a slower rise in food prices. There was a further slowdown in early 1971. The improvement proved to be short lived as the second quarter brought a rise of 5.3 percent (annual rate) in the CPI. Not only was there some stepup in the rise of food prices, but non food commodities also rose more rapidly, at about their 1970 rate.

Table 9.1
Changes in Consumer Prices for All Items
and All Items Less Food and Mortgage Interest*

		All Items	All Items Less Food and Interest Cost
December 1968	- December 1969	6.1	5.2
December 1969	- December 1970	5.5	5.9
December 1970	- March 1971	2.8	3.8
March 1971	- June 1971	5.3	6.1

* All inflation rates are annualized.

If food and interest rate effects are removed from the CPI, one gets a more accurate measure of prices which should directly respond to aggregate demand. Here the picture was not comforting to the stabilizers, as Table 9.1 shows. Except for the first quarter of 1971,

---

[2] *Economic Report of the President* (Washington, D.C., 1972), p. 41.

 Stabilization in the United States 1967-76

there was no deceleration in inflation at all. Keep in mind that all this was occurring at the same time that capacity utilization had fallen to 75 percent, and the unemployment rate had risen from 4 to 6 percent, hovering at the latter rate for the entire six-month period from December 1970 through May 1971. Orthodox policy was either not working to reduce expected inflation, or was working much more slowly than expected. With the 1972 election only a year away, political pressures mounted to try some other policy.

Even the economic advisers split. One group, pointing to the slow decline in the rate of increase of the CPI, contended that the stabilization was working and should be resolutely continued. A second group, headed by Arthur Burns, the new chairman of the Federal Reserve, argued that prices and wages were too unresponsive to demand conditions, and that a switch to an income policy— that is, some form of price and wage controls, must be considered. Here is Burns speaking in May 1971:[3]

> "During the past year and a half, our unemployment rate has risen from 3½ percent to about 6 percent. Labor is now readily available across the range of skills and in most sections of the country. Virtually, all industries have substantial amounts of excess capacity. In such circumstances, past experience would have led us to expect a substantial reduction in the rate of increase of costs and prices, if not actual declines. In fact, however, the improvement thus far has been modest. . . .
> Cost-push inflation cannot be dealt with effectively by using monetary and fiscal tools alone. In today's environment, efforts to do so would inevitably reduce output and employment far beyond the limits that our governments can accept or their citizens tolerate. On the other hand, I fear that cost pressures may become so intractable in our countries that they will ultimately weaken democratic institutions, besides stifling economic progress.
> Over a year ago, I reluctantly came to the conclusion that monetary and fiscal instruments needed to be supplemented for a time by incomes policy in the United States—that is, policies designed to enable labor and commodity markets to approximate more closely the competitive model."

[3] Arthur Burns, "Two Key Issues of Monetary Policy," *Federal Reserve Bulletin* (June 1971), 452–453.

    Inflation and Unemployment

Price and Wage Controls

In August 1971, confronted by a worsening balance of payments situation and inflationary recession at home, President Richard M. Nixon jettisoned his three-year-old stabilization program and embarked on the first peacetime price and wage controls in U.S. history. Unlike previous guidepost systems and many European incomes policies, the program was not voluntary. The price and wage ceilings had the force of law and violations could be rolled back and penalties could be assessed.

Phase I: August 15, 1971–November 14, 1971

Phase I of the program was a price and wage freeze for the ninety-day period August 15 through November 14, 1971. One of the main purposes of the freeze was to allow the authorities time to design a permanent program without allowing prices to rise in anticipation.

Phase II: November 15, 1971–January 11, 1973

The Phase II program set up a Cost of Living Council (CLC), which in turn delegated its authority to a number of different committees composed mainly of private citizens. The two most important were the Pay Board and the Price Commission. These two bodies were to set permissible standards for wages and prices and to decide their application in particular cases. Verification of compliance was left in the hands of the Internal Revenue Service.

The goal set by the CLC was to get the inflation rate down to 2–3 percent by the end of 1972. To this end the Pay Board set permissible wage increases for all workers at 5.5 percent. Since labor productivity on average had been growing at about 3 percent in the postwar period, this should have led to an inflation rate of 2.5 percent. Note that this rule gave all workers national average, rather than sectoral productivity, wage increases. Exceptions to the general ceilings were allowed for groups whose pay was grossly out of line with other comparable groups when the program began, and for workers whose pay had increased at less than 7 percent a year during the previous three years.

On the price side of the controls package, the general features were the following:

1. Firms were allowed to raise their prices by the same percentage amount that allowable costs had increased. Profits were therefore positively related to costs, as we pointed out in the last chapter.

2. Maximum profit margin rule: even if otherwise justified, price increases were not allowed if the firm's profit margin (profit as a percentage of sales) exceeded the average of the best two of the fiscal years preceding August 15, 1971.

3. Many large multiproduct firms were allowed to negotiate Term Limit Pricing (TLP) agreements with the Price Commission. These agreements specified a maximum by which the average of all the firm's prices might rise over the year. The TLP agreements set a maximum of 2 percent, which was later reduced to 1.8 percent. The idea was to relieve firms of the need to justify thousands of different price increases, each of which would require a complicated allocation of shared costs.

4. The intensity with which the program was enforced varied by the size of the firm. Firms were divided by size into three groups or tiers, and the large firms were subjected to closer surveillance and more stringent reporting requirements than the smaller ones.

The Council of Economic Advisers specifically denied that the size differentiated treatment stemmed from the inflationary bias of price-fixing in large firms with market power.[4] Still, the conventional wisdom of the advocates of controls was that price rigidity in the face of excess capacity was the cause of the difficulty in stopping inflation, and that inflexible prices, in turn, could be explained by markup pricing in industries dominated by big firms. The structure of the program was consistent with this approach.

Phase II lasted just over one year. On the surface its record was impressive. The inflation rate for 1972 fell to 3.4 percent from the 5–6 percent rate of the prefreeze period. At the same time, the authorities were emboldened by the presence of controls to abandon their restrictive fiscal and monetary policy. Fiscal policy was deliberately expansionary, and the money supply rose by 8.2 percent over the year 1972. In other words, the government shifted from orthodox restraint with no price or wage interference to price

---

[4] *Economic Report of the President* (Washington, D.C., 1973), p. 151.

and wage controls coupled with an expansionary monetary and fiscal policy. The results were heartening. At the same time that inflation seemed to be winding down, the unemployment rate fell from 6.1 percent to 5.1 percent, December 1971 to December 1972, and production rose by 7.6 percent. However, with the advantage of hindsight, it now appears that 1972's expansion was excessive. For the economy was sent, with wide open throttle, toward a rendezvous with a completely new economic problem—real scarcity. It was a problem that was to make a shambles of the controls program, and generate a new round of inflation far more virulent than anything seen in the United States up to that time.

By the end of 1972, with the economy heading toward full employment, the administrators of the controls program were anxious to modify it. Controls, they argued, are not particularly costly in a slack economy because changes in relative prices, which are necessary to retain the flexibility of a market economy, will not be great even in the absence of controls. But when the economy approaches capacity ceilings, all this changes. More essential commodities should have large relative price increases, either because they are relatively difficult to produce or difficult for consumers to replace. Thus, one would expect the price of oil, food, and housing to rise relative to speedboats, ski lift tickets, and large cars if the economy finds itself short of all six commodities. However, any price control system tends to freeze the price system of the economy into the pattern it had when the system started. Price signals to encourage a shift of production toward scarce commodities cannot occur. The longer the control system is in effect or the closer the economy is to full capacity, the more wasteful will be the errors in price setting by price administrators. For these reasons, the government changed the program in January 1973.

Phase III: January 11, 1973–June 1973

On January 11, 1973, in a masterpiece of bad timing, Phase III was announced. It was to last only until June. The big change in the new phase was a switch from a compulsory to a voluntary program. The government continued to set standards for "reasonable price and wage behavior" to which it requested that business and labor conform. No advance approval for price increases was required for the tier one firms. The government did, however, retain the legal right and the administrative ability to intervene where necessary. There was to be "a big stick in the closet." In only three sectors, food processing, construction, and health care were mandatory controls maintained. These were all sectors whose price indices had been rising at an uncomfortably rapid rate in 1972.

The new voluntary program appeared to be a disaster. The CPI, which had been so well behaved in 1972, began to rise—at an 8 percent rate during the first two quarters of 1973. The situation in the wholesale price index was equally bleak. Prices of crude industrial raw materials rose by 12 percent in just the first six months of 1973 (a 28 percent annual rate). Those are the prices which would be reflected in consumer prices with a three-to six-month lag. Thus no relief on the price front was in sight. A superficial observer of the economic situation would have concluded that the rapid expansion of 1972 had generated a new round of inflation.

A more careful look at the numbers reveals a rather different story. In Table 9.3 we show some of the components of the CPI and the WPI. It is clear from the table that the inflation was sector specific. It was occurring primarily in two sectors, food and crude materials for industry. In the uncomfortable first half of 1973, the prices of both food and industrial raw materials rose at about 25 percent annual rates. Such price behavior is unprecedented in the United States. What caused it? Was it the big increase in aggregate demand? My answer is no. While one can always say that demand conditions help determine the price level, in this case the data suggests that the basic problem was in supply.

Table 9.3
Sectoral Price Indices and Inflation Rates during 1973
(1967 = 100)

| | Components of WPI | | | | Components of CPI | |
| | Farm Products + Processed Feed | Crude Materials | Final Goods | | All Items | All Items Less Food |
			Producers	Consumer (excluding food)		
December 1972	132.6	136.8	120.3	114.6	127.3	127.6
March 1973	149.0	142.5	121.7	116.6	129.8	128.4
June 1973	163.6	152.8	123.4	118.4	132.4	130.3
September 1973	173.5	161.0	124.2	119.0	135.5	131.8
December 1973	168.0	179.8	126.7	123.1	138.5	134.8
Inflation rate in 1973	26.7%	31.4%	5.3%	7.4%	8.8%	5.0%

In the agricultural sector, a worldwide constellation of misfortunes combined to drastically reduce the supply of feed grains and meat.[5] The single most important event was a worldwide reduction of 36 million tons in the production of feed grains in 1972 due to crop problems in China, India and Russia. By the end of the year grain stocks had been reduced to minimal levels. The situation was complicated by a decline in the world production of animal feed supplements. In the United States, production of soybeans failed to expand significantly in 1972, partly because the farm price support program limited acreage planted. At the same time, the supply of fishmeal, an important feed supplement, was declining rapidly due to a fall of the catch of anchovies in Peru. The result was an explosion in feed grain prices. Soybeans rose from $120 per ton in March 1972 to $250 one year later. Livestock producers reacted by cutting production. By the beginning of 1973 some experts were warning that food prices would rise by 25 percent over the year. Their forecasts turned out to be conservative.

What are the explanations for the rapid rise in the prices of crude materials, including food? Largely they stem from a rapid rise in the prices of gasoline, copper, aluminum, lumber, and paper products.[6] The price increases for lumber, paper, and aluminum seem to be due to rapid increases in demand due to the rising level of economic activity and the construction boom in the United States. However, for petroleum refining, lumber and aluminum, part of the increase was due to the abnormally low rate of profit in 1970–72. These industries were allowed to raise prices to reestablish "normal" profit margins. Another important independent influence was the devaluation of the dollar in March. This made all imported commodities like oil, copper, and cotton more expensive, and raised the dollar price that foreigners were willing to pay for our food exports.

Meanwhile the price of other commodities and services that are important elements of the CPI continued to rise at about the same rates that they had in 1972. There was therefore a wide difference between sectoral inflation rates in the first six months of 1973 (see

---

[5] This selection relies heavily on John A. Schnittker, "The 1972–73 Food Price Spiral," *Brookings Papers on Economic Activity*, 2 (1973).

[6] Wholesale Prices and Price Indexes Data for July 1973.

Table 9.3). That fact suggests that generalized excess demand was not the principal culprit in the resurgence of inflation. The sectoral nature of inflation is also important to bear in mind when evaluating the success or lack of success of the wage and price control program. Not surprisingly, the renewal of strong inflationary pressure during 1973, immediately after the lifting of controls, led critics of the program to claim that controls had only delayed inflation. Supporters of controls countered that the new inflation gave added proof that more stringent controls were needed. However, I do not think that the sectoral behavior of prices during 1973 gives much support to either of these positions—namely, capacity limits in key sectors. We reserve discussion of this new problem and the anti-inflation policy it requires for later in the chapter. Here we return to the chronology of events in 1973.

As spring turned into summer, it was obvious that a major explosion in food and fuel prices was occurring. Despite the fact that the economy was in the midst of a runaway boom, pessimism, confusion and gloom prevailed over ways of containing the inflation. Finally in June the government caved in. Phase III's voluntary price program was unceremoniously abandoned and a new price freeze put in its place. The freeze lasted for two months and generated tremendous hostility in the agricultural sector. For the price freeze covered all processed food, but not grains and other livestock supplements. As we have already seen, key feeds had already doubled in price over the previous year. Now meat, eggs, milk and butter prices were not going to be allowed to reflect those cost increases. Livestock men cut back production and consumers read the sad news that pregnant sows were being slaughtered and young chicks being drowned.

Phase IV:
August 12, 1973–April 30, 1974 and Beyond

On August 12th, Phase IV was announced. In general design it was very similar to Phase II except for a more stringent rule for profits. Wage increases were held to a maximum of 5.5 percent per year plus .7 percent for fringe benefits. Price increases in the new phase were only allowed dollar for dollar with costs. If, for example, the wage bill for a firm was 50 percent of costs, and if wages rose by 5 percent, prices were allowed to go up by only 2.5 percent (.5 × .05) rather than 5 percent as in the Phase II program. Phase IV, in other words, instituted a profits freeze. Phase IV also required prenotification of price increases by all firms with more than 60 employees. Lumber, insurance, and regulated industries were exempted from controls. Over the remainder of the year a number of other industries were released from the program.

Phase IV was dominated by crop failures and the oil boycott. War broke out in the Middle East in the fall of 1973 and the Arabs imposed an oil boycott in November. Energy and food prices marched inexorably upward, drawing the inflation rate for the year to over 11 percent. Clearly no controls system could have worked under this combination of booming production and sectoral supply bottlenecks. Belatedly the government moved to reduce aggregate demand by a restrictive monetary and fiscal policy. The money supply fell 4.6 percent in real terms in 1974 and the full employment surplus rose by more than $35 billion. Most of this increase resulted from an inflation-caused increase in tax rates rather than any new tax or spending program.[7] Meanwhile, with the economy sliding into the sharpest recession of the postwar period, the wage and price controls system was quietly abandoned. Unemployment rates rose steadily throughout the unhappy year of 1974, peaking in May 1975 at the unprecedented level of 9 percent. Capacity utilization in manufacturing hit 71 percent, the lowest rate since the Korean War.

In response to this dismal situation, President Ford moved to a more expansionary stance. In March 1975 the Tax Reduction Act was passed. The money supply was allowed to expand as the Treasury paid out tax rebates in the second quarter, but then monetary authorities switched to a neutral or even contractionary policy. The economy responded to the stimulus, and by the fall of 1975 it was clear that a recovery was under way. Capacity utilization and production figures moved steadily upward through both 1976 and 1977. Despite its success in other areas, however, the recovery did not bring much relief from unemployment. The unemployment rate hovered at around 8 percent throughout 1976 and remained at over 7 percent in the fall of 1977, two years after the recovery got under way.

To recapitulate, on the output side, a recession cycle was started in late 1973, having its trough in May 1975. This cycle was the

---

[7] *Economic Report of the President* (Washington, D.C., 1976), p. 63.

intended result of demand management by the government. What was the result on the price front? As can be seen in Table 9.4, throughout the year 1974, the effects of the oil embargo and the food shortages rippled through the economy, with the inflation rate peaking at a 14.4 percent annual rate in the third quarter. Then as the recession began in earnest in 1975, the inflation rate fell back to the 7 percent range, where it has stayed ever since except for two quarters. It would thus appear that demand management was successful in limiting the oil-food price increases of 1973–74 to a temporary bulge of inflation.

In the 6–7 percent inflation range, however, the rates appear to be quite impervious to the level of aggregate demand. If one concentrates on the non-food component of the CPI in Table 9.4, as the set of prices which should be relatively sensitive to demand conditions, one can see that this index has continued to rise at around 6–7 percent since the first quarter of 1975, even though the economy has moved from recession to recovery. We will return to this point below. This means that the 1972 goal of bringing inflation down to 2–3 percent will not be achieved easily or cheaply. Thus, after so many anti-inflation programs and so many worker-years of employment lost, our stabilization is still not complete. Like so many other aspects of the Vietnam War, the inflation that it generated continues to plague us.

Thoughts on the Stabilization Period

What have we learned from the difficult and divisive experience of trying to stabilize the U.S. economy? These last seven years have seen the trial of practically all of the stabilization tools known to Western economists. We have tried surtaxes, tight money, wage controls, price controls, freezes, and guideposts. Can we draw any conclusions from our experiences?

The first and most important lesson we have learned is that orthodox demand reduction has only a weak effect on the rate of inflation, especially when the economy is operating at less than full employment. Experience bears out the contention of the ILM economists that the aggregate supply curve is kinked, and therefore that inflation rates tend to be inflexible downward. Tax surcharges and restrictive monetary policy successfully restrict

Table 9.4
Price Indices and Rates of Inflation Since 1973

	Price Indices (1967 = 100)		*Annualized Rates* [a]	
	CPI *All Items*	*CPI* *All Items Less Food*	*CPI* *All Items*	*CPI* *All Items Less Food*
3/73	129.8	128.4		
6/73	132.4	130.3	8.3	6.1
9/73	135.5	131.8	9.7	4.7
12/73	138.5	134.3	9.2	9.4
3/74	143.1	138.4	14.0	11.1
6/74	146.9	142.9	11.1	13.6
9/74	151.7	147.8	13.7	14.4
12/74	155.4	151.3	10.1	9.8
3/75	157.8	153.9	6.3	7.1
6/75	160.6	156.6	7.3	7.2
9/75	163.6	159.5	7.7	7.6
12/75	166.3	162.1	6.8	6.7
3/76	167.5	164.2	2.9	5.3
6/76	170.1	167.0	6.4	7.0
9/76	172.6	170.0	6.0	7.4
12/76	174.3	172.2	4.0	5.3
3/77	178.2	175.1	9.3	6.9
6/77	181.8	178.4	8.3	7.8

[a] Annualized rate is: $\left[\left(\dfrac{P_t}{P_{t-1}} \right)^4 - 1 \right] \times 100.$

Source: U.S. Department of Labor, Bureau of Labor Statistics.

aggregate demand, but output and employment fall far more sharply than the rate of inflation.

Twice during the ten-year stabilization, the government has caused recessions to stop inflation. The first time was in the years 1969–70 before price controls, and the second was just after the control system was abandoned, in mid-1974 through 1975. In neither case did inflation rates fall; once the capacity utilization rate fell below 85 percent. To show this visually we have plotted the rate of inflation of the non-food CPI against capacity utilization rates, quarter by quarter, for each of the stabilization periods (see Figures 9.1a and b). During 1973–74, the inflation rate was heavily influenced by the oil-food sector. Once that bulge was

  Stabilization in the United States 1967-76

worked off, inflation rates were virtually constant throughout 1976 and 1977, despite a variation in capacity utilization of over 13 percentage points. Figure 9.1a shows that in the 1968– 71 period, inflation rates were equally insensitive to variations in demand. Statistically, there is no relationship at all between the rate of inflation and capacity utilization at rates under 85 percent.

The Optimal Demand Curve

As we know, supporters of orthodox demand reduction to halt inflation base their policy on the upward sloping short-run supply curve. But the empirical evidence of these last years rather strongly supports the notion of a kinked supply curve, flat at less than some capacity utilization rate. If that is so, stabilization recessions are pointless. Suppose the kink occurs at or around an 85 percent utilization rate. Then it makes good sense to reduce demand to that level, but no sense at all to reduce it beyond that level. Those advisers who say that the rate of expansion of the money supply should be reduced or that the government deficit should be lowered, regardless of the circumstances, evidently believe that the aggregate supply curve is upward sloping throughout. But the evidence says that below some point, the supply curve changes shape and becomes flatter. Policymakers must adjust their policies to this change in conditions.

If the supply curve does have a kink, the goal of policymakers should be to make the demand curve intersect supply as close to the kink as possible (in region A of Figure 9.2). This will yield all the inflation abatement possible from demand management alone. In region C the economy will be subject to accelerating inflation, in region B to pointless recession (pointless in the sense that output is lost without producing a reduction in inflation rates). We do not know exactly the limits of region A, clearly an area for future research. But they undoubtedly lie somewhere in the range of 83– 87 percent of capacity utilization in manufacturing, which is a pretty broad target for government authorities to shoot at.

Other Lessons from Stabilization

Once again we learned, or were reminded, of the differential impact of stabilization. Demand reduction and

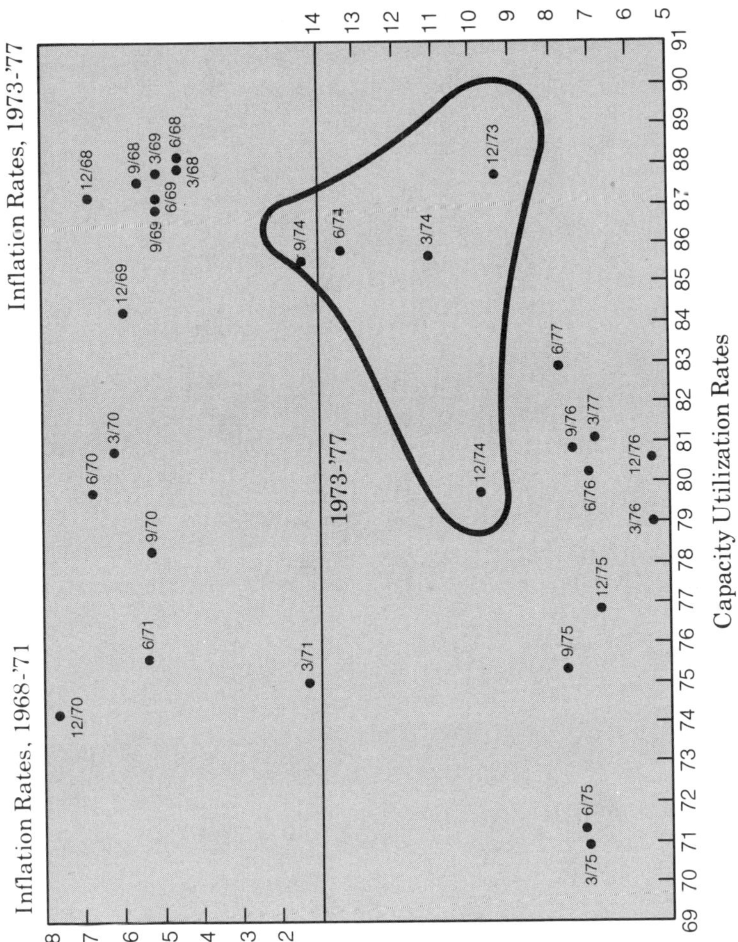

Inflation Rates, 1973-'77
Inflation Rates, 1968-'71
Capacity Utilization Rates
1973-'77
12/68
9/68
3/69
6/68
9/69
6/69
3/68
12/69
6/70
3/70
9/70
6/71
3/71
12/70
9/74
6/74
3/74
12/73
6/77
9/76
3/77
6/76
12/76
3/76
12/74
12/75
9/75
6/75
3/75
14
13
12
11
10
9
8
7
6
5
91 90 89 88 87 86 85 84 83 82 81 80 79 78 77 76 75 74 73 72 71 70 69
8
7
6
5
4
3
2

Figure 9.2
The Optimal Demand Curve

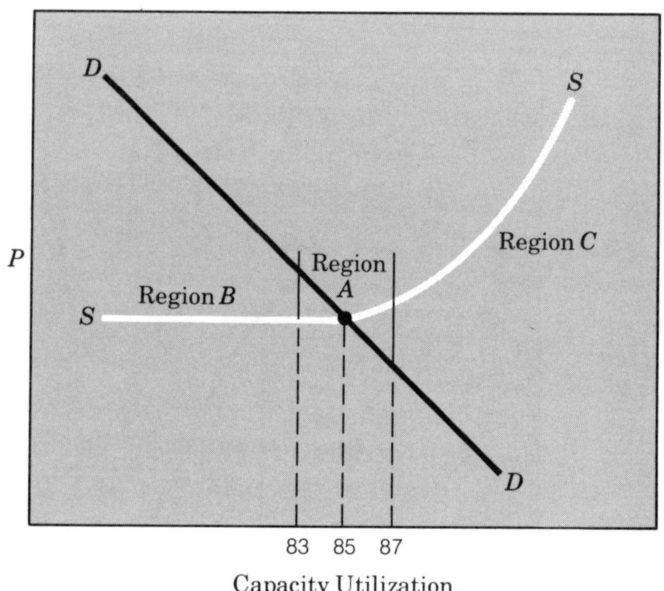

     Inflation and Unemployment

unemployment are not borne evenly by all sectors, but fall particularly hard on unskilled workers, the poor, and the young. At the height of the recession in 1975, the unemployment rate for married men was 5.8 percent. Meanwhile it was 21.8 percent for teenagers, 14.7 percent for blacks, 10.2 percent for women. Data on the earlier recession of 1970–71 shows an equal bias in the distribution of unemployment. As we saw in Chapter 7, the harsh distributional impacts of stabilization on the poor have been offset to some extent by an expansion in welfare payments. The verdict of the economic system has been partially set aside by transfers. Despite the rise in welfare payments, however, the distribution of income in the United States becomes less equal during the stabilization period. Some part of this is due to the differential impact of orthodox stabilization on different groups in the economy.

Thus U.S. experience leads us to fault orthodox stabilization on two grounds—efficiency and equity. It does not seem to stop inflation very well and its costs are borne to an inordinate degree by the poor and the unskilled. Advocates of such a policy should be required to provide a better justification for it than they have in the past, before we ever embark on another round of recession to stop inflation.

Economic historians looking back at the years 1971–74 will be searching for an answer to the question: were price controls effective, or what was the effect of controls? That is a very difficult question to answer because so many things were changing at the same time, and thus it is hard to identify the separate effects of the controls program. The fact that controls were established after two years of orthodox restraint further complicates the matter. If the rate of inflation went down during the control period, that could be nothing more than the lagged effect of the preceding policy. In order to prove that controls had an effect on the price level, one must construct a model of the U.S. economy, and let it generate the economic history which would have developed in the controls period had all policies other than controls been set at their historic levels. If such a simulated history showed a rate of inflation higher than the one actually observed, the controls had an effect. This has not been done to date, and the argument is at present inconclusive. The Council of Economic Advisers believes that controls had some effect in 1972, but academic opinion is mixed. Professor Gordon in a recent study estimates that controls may have reduced the inflation rate by as much as 2 percentage points.[8] Other researchers have found that the reductions in inflation during the control period are primarily explained by the previous reductions in the money supply and the level of aggregate demand.[9]

A number of people have argued that the imposition of controls only delayed inflation. As evidence for their position, they point to the outbreak of inflation in the first half of 1973 when controls were lifted. We have already described the particular sectoral composition of the inflation of that year. A closer look at patterns of price increases does not bear out the delayed inflation hypothesis. If price increases were delayed in the sectors where oligopoly firms have market power, we would expect these to be the sectors with high rates of inflation during the period of voluntary controls (Phase III: January 1973–June 1973). Yet the highly concentrated industries like machinery and chemicals do not show any significant rise in their inflation rates in this period.

A subtler argument is that the controls encouraged the authorities to adopt too expansionary a policy in 1972 and that this was responsible for the new inflation in 1973. There is some merit in this position. In 1972–73 the economy was pushed too hard, too fast. Capacity utilization surpassed 87 percent for the entire year of 1973. That is surely above the limits of the demand region consistent with constant inflation rates (region A of Figure 9.2). Probably there would have been less expansion in the absence of controls.

To sum up the discussion, there is no consensus of expert opinion on the net effect of the controls program. If controls did reduce the rate of inflation, the reductions were small and possibly due to other factors. Does this mean that the controls were a failure which should not be repeated? I do not believe so. In the first place, the existence of the controls program emboldened the government to

[8] Robert J. Gordon, "The Response of Wages and Prices to the First Two Years of Controls," *Brookings Papers on Economic Activity*, 3 (1973), 765–780.

[9] Edgar L. Feige and Douglas K. Pearce, "The Wage-Price Control Experiment—Did it Work?" *Challenge* (July-August 1973), 40–45.

     Inflation and Unemployment

abandon orthodox stabilization in 1972 and to push the economy to full employment. In my opinion, that should be counted as a plus for the program, even if the economy overshot its target.

Secondly, one should remember that the only policy alternatives to controls are 1) orthodox stabilization or 2) abandonment of the fight against inflation. As to the second, there does not appear to be any interest in adapting our system to permanent inflation through indexing,[10] so we are left really with a choice between orthodox stabilization and controls. No one likes controls, except perhaps some government bureaucrats. But one must remember that the alternative is induced recessions. Our experience in the United States suggests that an inflation curve via recession works terribly slowly, if it works at all. It entails literally billions of dollars of lost output and millions of worker years of unemployment. The greater the inflexibility of prices, the more costly is this type of anti-inflation program. In our economy prices appear to be quite inflexible downward. It is that fact which makes controls look like a "least bad" inflation cure.

Another lesson we learned from operating the controls program is that the distortions and misallocations of resources are much less serious when there is idle capacity. The price control system freezes relative prices, and that can have unforeseen and undesirable effects as the economy arrives at full capacity utilization. Several examples are sufficient to make the point. In the fuel industry, the August 1971 price freeze came when the price of gasoline was at a seasonal peak while fuel oil was at a seasonal low. Because of the controls, the latter was not allowed to rise the following winter. Naturally the refineries responded by switching production from fuel oil to gasoline, and the nation found itself with a fuel oil "shortage" that winter. It was not really a fuel shortage at all, just a misallocation of refinery capacity in response to an incorrect set of relative prices.

All of the difficulties with price setting should perhaps make us seriously consider the merits of a control program, based on tax penalties for excessive wage settlements. We discussed such a

---

10   Indexing means putting a cost-of-living clause into contracts which are written in money terms. This guarantees that an inflation during the life of the contract will not alter its real terms.

program in Chapter 8. While such a proposal may be politically unrealistic, there are also enormous political and economic costs attached to all the other alternatives as well. Few people want a complete price and wage control system, for then decisions which should be based on supply and demand become politicized. Having seen the political aspects of fuel pricing in the winters of 1973 and 1977, we should not have to emphasize such points. Probably fewer want the government to push us into another recession to stop inflation. Thus, the limited control program may be the least costly way to escape from an inflation, both economically and politically.

Finally, 1973 seems to me to be the first taste of a new phenomenon—sectoral scarcities leading to secoral, or supply, inflation. As I have indicated above, I think that the excess demand which drove prices up in 1973–74 was not general, but was sector-specific. What are the appropriate policies for such an inflation?

Certainly price controls are not likely to be effective. We have already seen the damages they can cause when there are capacity constraints. The fact is that relative prices of the scarce commodities *must* rise. That is the only way to increase their supply and induce consumers to substitute less scarce commodities for them. If other prices are inflexible downward, policymakers are faced with a dilemma. They can ratify the sectoral price increases by expansionary policy, or try to force other prices to fall far enough to offset the prices which are rising. But our experience suggests that prices are inflexible downward beyond a certain point. Therefore demand constraint to stop a sectoral inflation will simply result in recession in the rest of the economy. Business will find that high energy or food prices are cutting into its sales of other commodities. In my opinion, the costs in unemployment and lost output are simply too high to make demand constraint beyond the 83–87 percent capacity range an acceptable method of controlling this sort of inflation. In the short run an inflation resulting from energy shortages should be accepted. In the long run the only alternative is to increase research and investment so as to replace with produced capital the scarce resources that have been depleted by use. The economic system is capable of adjusting to this new challenge if we have the patience and forbearance to realize that the adjustment is going to take time, and that during that time, we should expect and prepare for a certain amount of inflation. Indeed, with inflexible prices, inflation is a strong indicator that the adjustment is taking place.

Questions

1. The U.S. economy seems to be "stuck" at an inflation rate of around 6 percent, despite the best efforts of the government to drive it to lower levels. What are possible explanations for this, and what if anything would you recommend that the government do about it?
2. Many people think that inflation is caused by government deficit spending. Do you agree? If so, why? If not, why not?
3. Milton Friedman has said that all inflations are caused by too fast an increase in the money supply. If that is true, can we reduce the inflation rate by slowing the rate of expansion in the money supply?
4. Is taxation as an anti-inflationary tool doomed to practical ineffectiveness because of the long time lag between the need for the tax and the passage of the tax law? Do you have any recommendations about how the time lag could be shortened?
5. Does a rise in the price of an important commodity, such as oil, necessarily lead to a rise in the price level?
6. Wage and price controls have clearly been effective in the United States because the rate of inflation fell after they were imposed and rose after they were removed. Discuss.
7. The expectations model of inflation offers an explanation for the high rates of unemployment of recent years. What is that explanation, and is it consistent with evidence from the labor market?

Suggestions for Further Reading

Bosworth, Barry, "Phase II: The U.S. Experiment with an Incomes Policy," *Brookings Papers on Economic Activity*, 2 (1972).

Cagan, Phillip, *et al.*, *A New Look at Inflation.* Washington, D.C.: American Enterprise Institute, 1973.

Goodwin, Craufurd D., ed., *Exhortation and Controls*. Washington, D.C.: The Brookings Institution, 1975.

Gordon, Robert A., "The Response of Wages and Prices to the First Two Years of Controls," *Brookings Papers on Economic Activity*, 3 (1973), 765–780.

Hall, Robert E., "The Rigidity of Wages and the Persistence of Unemployment," *Brookings Papers on Economic Activity*, 2 (1975), 301–351.

Lanzilotti, Robert F., *et al., Phase II in Review–The Price Commission Experience*. Washington, D.C.: The Brookings Institution, 1975.

Poole, William, "Wage-Price Controls: Where Do We Go From Here?" *Brookings Papers on Economic Activity*, 1 (1973), 285–303.

Schnittker, John A., "The 1972–73 Food Price Spiral," *Brookings Papers on Economic Activity*, 2 (1973), 498–508.

Weber, Arnold R., *In Pursuit of Price Stability*. Washington, D.C.: The Brookings Institution, 1973.

Appendix A
Tables

Table A.1
Prices, 1950–1970 (1967 = 100)
Consumer Price Indices, by Major Groups

Year	All Items	Food	Housing Total	Housing Rent	Apparel and Upkeep	Transportation	Medical Care	Personal Care	Reading and Recreation	Other Goods and Services
1950	72.1	74.5	72.8	70.4	79.0	68.2	53.7	68.3	74.4	69.9
1951	77.8	82.8	77.2	73.2	86.1	72.5	56.3	74.7	76.6	72.8
1952	79.5	84.3	78.7	76.2	85.3	77.3	59.3	75.6	76.9	76.6
1953	80.1	83.0	80.8	80.3	84.6	79.5	61.4	76.3	77.7	78.5
1954	80.5	82.8	81.7	83.2	84.5	78.3	63.4	76.6	76.9	79.8
1955	80.2	81.6	82.3	84.3	84.1	77.4	64.8	77.9	76.7	79.8
1956	81.4	82.2	83.6	85.9	85.8	78.8	67.2	81.1	77.8	81.0
1957	84.3	84.9	86.2	87.5	87.3	83.3	69.9	84.1	80.7	83.3
1958	86.6	88.5	87.7	89.1	87.5	86.0	73.2	86.9	83.9	84.4
1959	87.3	87.1	88.6	90.4	88.2	89.6	76.4	88.7	85.3	86.1
1960	88.7	88.0	90.2	91.7	89.6	89.6	79.1	90.1	87.3	87.8
1961	89.6	89.1	90.9	92.9	90.4	90.6	81.4	90.6	89.3	88.5
1962	90.6	89.9	91.7	94.0	90.9	92.5	83.5	92.2	91.3	89.1
1963	91.7	91.2	92.7	95.0	91.9	93.0	85.6	93.4	92.8	90.6
1964	92.9	92.4	93.8	95.9	92.7	94.3	87.3	94.5	95.0	92.0
1965	94.5	94.4	94.9	96.9	93.7	95.9	89.5	95.2	95.9	94.2
1966	97.2	99.1	97.2	98.2	96.1	97.2	93.4	97.1	97.5	97.2
1967	100.0	100.0	100.0	100.0	100.0	100.0	100.0	100.0	100.0	100.0
1968	104.2	103.6	104.2	102.4	105.4	103.2	106.1	104.2	104.7	104.6
1969	109.8	108.9	110.8	105.7	111.5	107.2	113.4	109.3	108.7	109.1
1970	116.3	114.9	118.9	110.1	116.1	112.7	120.6	113.2	113.4	116.0
1971	121.3	118.4	124.3	115.2	119.8	118.6	128.4	116.8	119.3	120.9
1972	125.3	123.5	129.2	119.2	122.3	119.9	132.5	119.8	122.8	125.5
1973	133.1	141.4	135.0	124.3	126.8	123.8	137.7	125.2	125.9	129.0
1974	147.7	161.7	150.6	130.6	136.2	137.7	150.5	137.3	133.8	137.2
1975	161.2	175.4	166.8	137.3	142.3	150.6	168.6	150.7	144.4	147.4
1976	170.5	180.8	177.2	144.7	147.6	165.5	184.7	160.5	151.2	153.3
1977	181.5	192.2	189.6	153.5	154.2	177.2	202.4	170.9	157.9	159.2

Source for all tables in the Appendix is: United States Government, *Economic Report of the President – 1978,* Washington, D.C.: U.S. Government Printing Office, 1978.

   Inflation and Unemployment

Table A. 2
Rates of Inflation, 1950–1977
(annual percentage changes)

Year	Consumer Price Index	Wholesale Price Index	GDP Deflator
1950	1.0	3.9	2.0
1951	7.9	11.4	6.7
1952	2.2	− 2.7	1.3
1953	0.8	− 1.4	1.5
1954	0.5	0.2	1.4
1955	− 0.4	0.2	2.2
1956	1.5	3.3	3.2
1957	3.6	2.9	3.4
1958	2.7	1.4	1.6
1959	0.8	0.2	2.2
1960	1.6	0.1	1.7
1961	1.0	− 0.4	0.9
1962	1.1	0.3	1.9
1963	1.2	− 0.3	1.5
1964	1.3	0.2	1.6
1965	1.7	2.0	2.2
1966	2.9	3.3	3.3
1967	2.8	0.2	3.0
1968	4.2	2.5	4.5
1969	5.4	3.9	5.1
1970	5.7	3.7	5.3
1971	4.3	3.2	5.1
1972	3.3	4.5	4.1
1973	6.2	13.1	5.7
1974	11.0	18.9	5.5
1975	9.1	9.2	9.7
1976	5.8	4.6	5.2
1977	6.5	6.1	5.5

Table A. 3
National Accounts, 1950–1977
(billions of dollars, 1972 prices)

| Year | GNP | Disposable Personal Income | Personal Consumption | Private Domestic Investment | Government Expenditures | | Exports | Imports |
					Federal	State & Local		
1950	533.5	205.5	338.1	93.7	47.0	50.7	21.7	17.7
1955	654.8	273.4	395.1	104.1	86.9	64.0	27.9	23.2
1960	736.8	349.4	453.0	105.4	90.8	82.0	35.8	30.3
1961	755.3	362.9	462.2	103.6	95.6	87.1	37.0	30.3
1962	799.1	383.9	482.9	117.4	103.1	90.0	39.6	33.9
1963	830.7	402.8	501.4	124.5	102.2	95.4	42.2	35.0
1964	874.4	437.0	528.7	132.1	100.6	102.1	47.8	36.9
1965	925.9	472.2	558.1	150.1	100.5	109.1	49.1	41.0
1966	981.0	510.4	586.1	161.3	112.5	116.8	51.6	47.3
1967	1007.0	544.5	603.2	152.7	125.3	123.1	54.2	50.7
1968	1051.8	588.1	633.4	159.5	128.3	130.9	58.5	58.9
1969	1078.8	630.4	655.4	168.0	121.8	134.9	62.2	63.5
1970	1075.3	685.9	668.9	154.7	110.7	139.5	67.1	65.7
1971	1107.5	742.8	691.9	166.8	103.9	145.5	67.9	68.5
1972	1171.1	801.3	733.0	188.3	102.1	151.0	72.7	75.9
1973	1235.0	901.7	767.7	207.2	96.6	155.9	87.4	79.9
1974	1217.8	984.6	760.7	183.6	95.8	161.8	93.0	77.1
1975	1202.1	1084.4	775.1	141.6	96.7	166.3	89.9	67.4
1976	1274.7	1185.8	821.3	173.0	96.5	167.9	95.8	79.8
1977	1337.6	1308.6	860.3	195.6	101.4	169.7	98.0	77 3

  Inflation and Unemployment

Table A. 4
Labor Market Data

Year	Unemployment Rates (workers)	Real Wages[1]	Index of Labor Cost Per Dollar[2] of Sales	Index of Total Real Compensation Per Hour, 1967=100
1950	5.3%	$ 73.69	98.1	64.4
1951	3.3	74.37	98.3	65.6
1952	3.0	76.29	99.5	67.8
1953	2.9	79.60	101.5	70.3
1954	5.5	80.15	101.9	71.7
1955	4.4	84.44	99.3	72.7
1956	4.1	86.90	101.7	74.9
1957	4.3	86.99	101.9	76.8
1958	6.8	86.70	102.5	78.8
1959	5.5	90.24	100.7	80.2
1960	5.5	90.95	102.8	82.6
1961	6.7	92.19	102.6	84.8
1962	5.5	94.82	101.7	87.7
1963	5.7	96.47	100.5	89.9
1964	5.2	98.31	100.1	92.7
1965	4.5	100.59	98.8	94.6
1966	3.8	101.67	99.4	97.6
1967	3.8	101.84	100.0	100.0
1968	3.6	103.39	99.9	103.1
1969	3.5	104.38	101.8	105.0
1970	4.9	102.72	103.5	106.8
1971	5.9	104.93	102.4	108.9
1972	5.6	108.67	102.0	111.7
1973	4.9	109.26	103.8	115.7
1974	5.6	104.57	106.0	114.0
1975	8.5	101.67	103.8	113.6
1976	7.7	103.40	102.4	117.0
1977	7.0	104.22	103.2	120.4

[1] Average gross weekly earnings, 1967 prices, total private non-farm.
[2] Wages and salaries of employees in private non-farm business plus employers' contributions for social insurance and private benefit plans, deflated by implicit price deflator for total private non-farm business.

     Appendix A / Tables

Table A. 5
Factor Shares, 1950–1977

Year	Total Wage Income as a Percent of National Income	Corporation Profits Before Taxes as a Percent of National Income*
1950	65.5%	14.3%
1951	66.5	14.0
1952	68.5	12.4
1953	69.9	11.8
1954	69.7	11.6
1955	68.6	13.6
1956	70.2	12.4
1957	70.8	11.6
1958	70.9	10.3
1959	70.4	12.1
1960	71.6	11.3
1961	71.6	11.1
1962	71.1	12.0
1963	71.0	12.3
1964	70.9	12.9
1965	70.1	13 6
1966	70.6	13.3
1967	72.0	12.1
1968	72.8	12.0
1969	74.4	10.6
1970	76.3	8.5
1971	75.8	9.0
1972	75.1	9.7
1973	75.1	9.3
1974	77.1	7.4
1975	76.4	8.2
1976	76.0	9.4
1977	76.0	9.2

* Includes inventory valuation adjustment.

Table A. 6
Fiscal and Monetary Data

Year	Money Supply* (billions of dollars, 1967 prices)	Federal Government Receipts as a Percent of GNP	State and Local Government Receipts as a Percent of GNP
1950	161.2	17.5%	7.4%
1955	168.6	18.2	7.9
1960	162.6	19.0	9.9
1961	166.0	18.7	10.3
1962	166.6	18.8	10.4
1963	170.7	19.2	10.6
1964	176.2	18.1	10.9
1965	181.3	18.1	10.9
1966	180.8	18.8	11.3
1967	192.7	19.0	11.8
1968	202.2	20.1	12.3
1969	200.4	21.1	12.8
1970	200.0	19.5	13.7
1971	201.0	18.7	14.4
1972	210.5	19.4	15.1
1973	203.2	19.8	14.8
1974	191.7	20.4	14.9
1975	182.9	18.9	15.5
1976	183.2	19.5	15.5
1977	184.8	19.8	15.6

*Average December currency supply plus demand deposits divided by December CPI, 1967 = 100.

Table A. 7
International Consumer Price Indices, 1960–1977
(1967 = 100)

Year	United States	Canada	Japan	France	Germany	Italy	United Kingdom
1960	88.7	85.9	67.7	78.8	82.8	74.1	78.9
1961	89.6	86.7	71.3	81.4	84.7	75.7	81.6
1962	90.6	87.7	76.1	85.3	87.3	79.2	85.1
1963	91.7	89.3	81.9	89.4	89.8	85.1	86.8
1964	92.9	90.9	85.0	92.5	92.0	90.1	89.6
1965	94.5	93.1	91.5	94.8	94.9	94.2	93.9
1966	97.2	96.6	96.2	97.4	98.3	96.4	97.6
1967	100.0	100.0	100.0	100.0	100.0	100.0	100.0
1968	104.2	104.1	105.3	104.5	101.5	101.4	104.7
1969	109.8	108.8	110.8	111.3	103.4	104.1	110.4
1970	116.3	112.4	119.3	117.1	107.0	109.2	117.4
1971	121.3	115.6	126.8	123.5	112.6	114.5	128.5
1972	125.3	121.1	133.0	131.1	118.9	121.0	137.6
1973	133.1	130.3	148.5	140.7	127.1	134.2	150.3
1974	147.7	144.5	183.0	160.0	136.0	159.8	174.3
1975	161.2	160.1	204.5	178.9	144.1	186.9	216.5
1976	170.5	172.1	223.7	196.1	150.6	218.2	252.4
1977	181.5	. . . . .	. . . . .	. . . . .	. . . . .	. . . . .	. . . . .

 Inflation and Unemployment